Getting Started with MATLAB

A Quick Introduction
for Scientists and Engineers

Disclaimer

Under no circumstances does
the author assume any responsibility
and liability thereof, for any injury caused
to the reader by toxic fumes and explosions
resulting from mixing incompatible matrices and
vectors. Array operations are known to cause
irritability and minor itching to beginners. The author,
however, might buy the reader a cup of coffee in the
case of serious distress. In rare cases of very flattering
comments or very creative suggestions about
improving this book, the author might even buy
the reader lunch. The reader is encouraged to
try his/her luck by sending comments
to rp28@cornell.edu.

Getting Started with

M A T L A B®

A Quick Introduction for
Scientists and Engineers

RUDRA PRATAP, **Ph.D.**
Theoretical and Applied Mechanics
Cornell University

Saunders Golden Sunburst Series

Saunders College Publishing
HARCOURT BRACE COLLEGE PUBLISHERS

Fort Worth   Philadelphia   San Diego   New York   Orlando   Austin
San Antonio   Toronto   Montreal   London   Sydney   Tokyo

Pratap; Getting Started With Matlab

ISBN 0-03-017884-3

567 017 987654321

To Ma Gayatri

and my parents
Shri Chandrama Singh and Smt. Bachcha Singh

Contents

Preface

I enjoy MATLAB, and I want you to enjoy it too—that is the singular motivation behind this book. The first and foremost goal of this book is to get you started in MATLAB quickly and pleasantly.

Learning MATLAB changed the meaning of scientific computing for me. I used to think in terms of machine-specific compilers and tables of numbers as output. Now, I expect and enjoy interactive calculation, programming, graphics, animation, and complete portability across platforms—all under one roof. MATLAB is simple, powerful, and for most purposes quite fast. This is not to say that MATLAB is free of quirks and annoyances. It is not a complete miracle drug, but I like it and I think you will probably like it too.

I first used MATLAB seven years ago in a course on matrix computation taught by Tom Coleman. We used the original 1984 commercial version of MATLAB. Although the graphics capability was limited to bare-bones 2-D plots, and programming was not possible on the mainframe VAX, I still loved it. After that I used MATLAB in every course I took. I did all the computations for my Ph.D. dissertation in nonlinear dynamics using MATLAB. Since then I have used MATLAB in every engineering and mathematics course I have taught. I have enthusiastically tried to teach MATLAB to my friends, colleagues, students, and my 14-month-old daughter. I have given several introductory lectures, demonstrations, and hands-on workshops. This book is a result of my involvement with MATLAB teaching, both informal and in the class room, over the last seven years.

This book is intended to get you started quickly. After an hour or two of getting started you can use the book as a reference. There are many examples, which you can modify for your own use. The coverage of topics is based on my experience of what is most useful, and what I wish I could have found in a book when I was learning MATLAB. If you find the book informative and useful, it is my pleasure to be of service to you. If you find it frustrating, please share your frustrations with me so that I can try to improve future editions.

1

Acknowledgments.

I was helped through the development of this book by the encouragement, criticism, editing, typing, and test-learning of many people. I thank all students who have used this book in its past forms and provided constructive criticism. Among my colleagues, Chris Wohlever, Mike Coleman, John Abel, and Richard Rand have always provided encouragement. Andy Ruina has has been an integral part of the development of this book all along, his criticisms and suggestions have influenced every page. I am grateful to Christopher D. Hall, Air Force Institute of Technology; James R. Wohlever, Western Connecticut State University, John T. Demel; the Ohio State University; Jeffrey L. Cipolla, Naval Undersea Warfare Center; John C. Polking, Rice University; and people at MathWorks Inc., especially Cristina Palumbo, for helpful reviews of the first draft of the book. I am thankful to John Gibson for reading and editing the entire manuscript. Many thanks to my editor Sara Tenney and the Saunders production staff who have made this glossy-cover version possible.

I am grateful to my mother-in-law, Mrs. Usharani Nayak, whose visit during the Fall of 1994 enabled the writing of the first full-size draft (I got the time while she played with her four-month-old granddaughter). Lastly, if it wasn't for the infinite patience of my wife, Kalpana, with all the stress of finishing her own Ph.D. thesis and taking care of little Manisha during the past several months, this book would have never gotten into or out of my computer.

Thank you all.

Ithaca, NY   Rudra Pratap.
July, 1995.

1. *Introduction*

1.1 What Is MATLAB?

MATLAB™ is a software package for high-performance numerical computation and visualization. It provides an interactive environment with hundreds of built-in functions for technical computation, graphics, and animation. Best of all, it also provides easy extensibility with its own high-level programming language. The name MATLAB stands for MATrix LABoratory.

The diagram in Fig. 1.1 shows the main features and capabilities of MATLAB. MATLAB's built-in functions provide excellent tools for linear algebra computations, data analysis, signal processing, optimization, numerical solution of ODEs, quadrature, and many other types of scientific computations. Most of these functions use state-of-the art algorithms. There are numerous functions for 2-D and 3-D graphics as well as for animation. Also, for those who cannot do without their Fortran or C codes, MATLAB even provides an external interface to run those programs from within MATLAB. The user, however, is not limited to the built-in functions; he can write his own functions in MATLAB language. Once written, these functions behave just like the built-in functions. MATLAB's language is very easy to learn and to use.

There are also several *optional* 'Toolboxes' available from the developers of MATLAB. These Toolboxes are collections of functions written for special applications such as Symbolic Computation, Image Processing, Statistics, Control System Design, and Neural Networks.

3

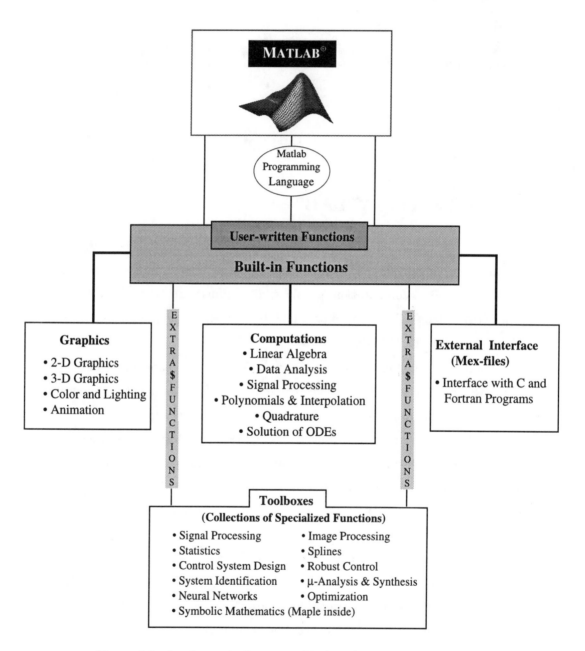

Figure 1.1: A schematic diagram of MATLAB's main features.

The basic building block of MATLAB is the matrix. The only data type is complex matrix [1] and you never need to declare it. Vectors, scalars, real matrices and integer matrices are all *automatically* handled as special cases of the basic data type. What is more, you almost never have to declare the dimensions of a matrix. MATLAB simply loves matrices and matrix operations. The built-in functions are optimized for vector operations. Consequently, *vectorized* commands or codes run much faster in MATLAB.

1.2 Does MATLAB Do Symbolic Calculations?

(MATLAB vs Mathematica, Maple, Macsyma, and MathCad)

If you are new to MATLAB, you are likely to ask this question. The first thing to realize is that MATLAB is primarily a numerical computation package, although with the Symbolic Toolbox (standard with the Student Edition of MATLAB) it can do symbolic algebra [2]. Mathematica, Maple, and Macsyma are primarily symbolic algebra packages. Of course, they do numerical computations too. In fact, if you know any of these packages *really* well, you can do almost every calculation that MATLAB does using that software. So why learn MATLAB? Well, MATLAB's ease of use is its best feature. Also, it has a shallow learning curve (more learning with less effort) while the computer algebra systems have a steep learning curve. Since MATLAB was primarily designed to do calculations and computer algebra systems were not, MATLAB is often much faster at calculations—often as fast as C or Fortran. MathCad, however, is closer in aim and scope, but it falls far short in terms of extendability. MathCad lacks a programming environment. There are other packages, such as Matrix X for Unix workstations, that are also closer in aim and scope but are limited to a particular platform. The bottom line is, in numerical computations, especially those that utilize vectors and matrices, MATLAB beats everyone hands down in terms of ease of use, availability of built-in functions, ease of programming, and speed. The proof is in the phenomenal growth of MATLAB users around the country and the world in just a few years. There are more than

---

[1] This is not quite true although MathWorks claims so. There are data-objects, such as character strings and functions, that are different data-type. Although there is no explicit data-type declaration for such objects, they are *sneaked in* differently.

[2] Symbolic algebra means that computation is done in terms of symbols or variables rather than numbers. For example, if you type (x+y)^2 on your computer and the computer responds by saying that the expression is equal to $x^2 + 2xy + y^2$, then your computer does symbolic algebra. Software packages that do symbolic algebra are also known as *Computer Algebra Systems*.

2500 universities and thousands of companies listed as registered users. MATLAB's popularity today has forced such powerful packages as Mathematica and Macsyma to provide extensions for files in MATLAB's format!

1.3 Will MATLAB Run on My Computer?

The most likely answer is "yes," because MATLAB supports almost every computational platform. In addition to PCs and Macintosh computers, versions are available for Sun SPARCstations, HP 9000 Series 700, IBM RS/6000, Silicon Graphics IRIS Series 4D, DEC RISC, DEC Alpha workstations, VAX computers, and even CRAY supercomputers.

1.4 Where Do I Get MATLAB?

MATLAB is a product of the MathWorks, Incorporated. Contact the company for product information and ordering at the following address.

The MathWorks Inc.
24 Prime Park Way, Natick MA 01760
Phone: (508) 653-1415,   Fax: (508) 653-2997.
Email: info@mathworks.com
World Wide Web: http://www.mathworks.com

1.5 How Do I Use This Book?

This book is intended to serve as an introduction to MATLAB. All features are discussed through examples following these conventions:

- **Typographical styles:**

    - All actual MATLAB commands or instructions are shown in `typed face`.

    - Place holders for variables or names in a command are shown in *italics*. So, a command shown as `help` *topic* implies that you have to type the actual name of a topic in place of *topic* in the command.

    - *Italic* text has also been used to *emphasize* a point and sometimes, to introduce a new term.

- **Actual examples:** Actual examples carried out in MATLAB are shown in gray, shaded boxes. Explanatory notes have been added within small white rectangles in the gray boxes as shown below.

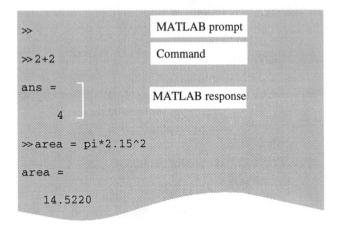

Figure 1.2: Actual examples carried out in MATLAB are shown in gray boxes throughout this book. The texts in the white boxes inside these gray boxes are explanatory notes.

These gray, boxed figures are intended to provide a parallel track for the impatient reader. If you would rather try out MATLAB right away, you are encouraged to go through these boxed examples. Most of the examples are designed so that you can (more or less) follow them without reading the entire text. All examples are system-independent. After trying out the examples, you should read the appropriate sections.

- **On-line help** We encourage the use of on-line help. For almost all major topics, we indicate the on-line help *category* in a small box in the margin as shown here.

On-line help category: `help`

Typing `help` *category* in MATLAB with the appropriate category name provides a list of functions and commands in that category. Detailed help can then be obtained for any of those commands and functions.

We discourage a passive reading of this book. The best way to learn any computer software is to try it out. We believe this, practice it, and encourage you to practice it too. So, if you are impatient, quickly read Sections 1.6.1–1.6.3, jump to the tutorials on page 15, and get going.

1.6   Basics of MATLAB

Here we discuss some basic features and commands. To begin, let us look at the general structure of the MATLAB environment.

1.6.1   MATLAB windows

On all Unix systems, Macs, and PCs, MATLAB works through three basic windows, which are shown in Fig. 1.3 and discussed below.

1. **Command window:** This is the main window. It is characterized by the MATLAB prompt '≫'. When you launch the application program, MATLAB puts you in this window. All commands, including those for running user-written programs, are typed in this window at the MATLAB prompt.

2. **Graphics window:** The output of all graphics commands typed in the command window are flushed to the graphics or *Figure* window, a separate window with (default) black background color. The user can create as many figure windows as the system memory will allow.

3. **Edit window:** This is where you write, edit, create, and save your own programs in files called '*M-files*'. You can use any text editor to carry out these tasks. On some systems, such as Macs, MATLAB provides its own built-in editor. On other systems, you can invoke the edit window by typing the standard file-editing command that you normally use on your system. The command is typed at the MATLAB prompt following the special character '!'. The exclamation character prompts MATLAB to return the control temporarily to the local operating system, which executes the command following the '!' character. After the editing is completed, the control is returned to MATLAB. For example, on Unix systems, typing `!vi myprogram.m` at the MATLAB prompt (and hitting the return key at the end) invokes the `vi` editor on the file 'myprogram.m'. Typing `!emacs myprogram.m` invokes the emacs editor.

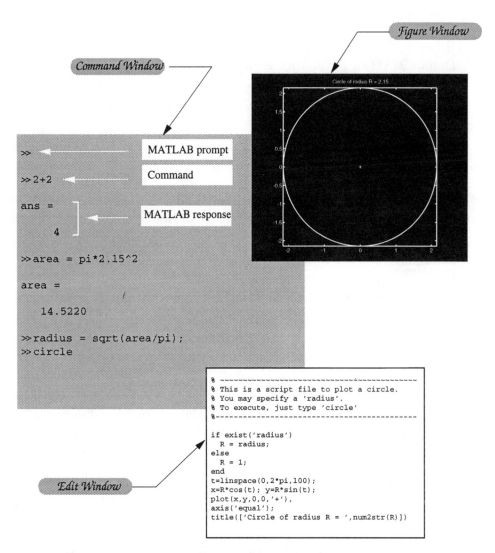

Figure 1.3: The MATLAB environment consists of a Command Window, a Figure Window, and a platform-dependent Edit Window.

1.6.2 On-line help

- **On-line documentation:** MATLAB provides on-line help for all its built-in functions and programming language constructs. The commands `help` and `lookfor` provide on-line help. See Section 3.3 for a description of the help facility.

- **Demo:** MATLAB has a demonstration program that shows many of its features. The program includes a tutorial introduction that is worth trying. Type `expo` at the MATLAB prompt to invoke the demonstration program, and follow the instructions on the screen.

1.6.3 Input-Output

MATLAB supports interactive computation (see Chapter 3), taking the input from the screen, and flushing the output to the screen. In addition, it can read input files and write output files (see Section 4.4.7). The following features hold for all forms of input-output:

- **Data type**: Basically, there is only one data type in MATLAB: *complex matrix*, real numbers and integers are special cases. For example, there is no need to declare variables as real. When a real number is entered as the value of a variable, MATLAB automatically sets the imaginary part to zero.

- **Dimensioning:** Dimensioning is automatic in MATLAB. No dimension statements are required for vectors or arrays. You can find the dimensions of an existing matrix or a vector with the `size` and `length` (for vectors only) commands.

- **Case sensitivity:** MATLAB is case-sensitive; that is, it differentiates between the lowercase and uppercase letters. Thus a and A are different variables. Most MATLAB commands and built-in function calls are typed in lowercase letters. You can turn case sensitivity on and off with the `casesen` command.

- **Output display:** The output of every command is displayed on the screen unless MATLAB is directed otherwise. A semicolon at the end of a command suppresses the screen output, except in the cases of graphics and on-line help commands. The following facilities are provided for controlling the screen output:

- **Paged output:** To direct MATLAB to show one screen of output at a time, type `more on` at the MATLAB prompt. Without it, MATLAB flushes the entire output at once, without regard to the speed at which you read.

- **Output format:** Though computations inside MATLAB are done using double precision, the appearance of floating point numbers on the screen is controlled by the output `format` in use. There are several different screen output formats. The following table shows the printed value of 10π in 7 different formats.

```
format short        31.4159
format short e      3.1416e+01
format long         31.41592653589793
format long e       3.141592653589793e+01
format hex          403f6a7a2955385e
format rat          3550/113
format bank         31.42
```

The additional formats `format compact` and `format loose` control the spacing above and below the displayed numbers, and `format +` displays a `+`, `-`, and blank for positive, negative, and zero numbers, respectively. The default is `format short`. The display format is set by typing `format` *type* on the command line.

- **Command history:** MATLAB saves previously typed commands in a buffer. These commands can be recalled with the **up-arrow** key (↑). This helps in editing previous commands. You can also recall a previous command by typing the first few characters and then pressing the ↑ key. On most Unix systems, MATLAB's command-line editor also understands the standard emacs keybindings.

1.6.4 File types

MATLAB has three types of files for storing information:

M-files are standard ASCII text files, with a `.m` extension to the filename. There are two types of these files: *script files* and *function files* (see Section 4.1 and 4.2). Most programs you write in MATLAB are saved as M-files. All built-in functions in MATLAB are M-files, most of which reside on your computer in precompiled format. Some built-in functions are provided with source code in readable M-files so that they can be copied and modified.

Mat-files are binary data-files, with a `.mat` extension to the filename. Mat-files are created by MATLAB when you save data with the `save` command. The data is written in a special format that only MATLAB can read. Mat-files can be loaded into MATLAB with the `load` command (see Section 3.4 for details.).

Mex-files are MATLAB -callable Fortran and C programs, with a `.mex` extension to the filename. Use of these files requires some experience with MATLAB and a lot of patience. We do not discuss Mex-files in this introductory book.

1.6.5   Platform dependence

One of the best features of MATLAB is its platform-independence. Once you are in MATLAB, for most part, it does not matter which computer you are on. Almost all commands work the same way. The only commands that differ are the ones that necessarily depend on the local operating system, such as editing and saving M-files. Programs written in the MATLAB language work exactly the same way on all computers. The user interface (how you interact with your computer), however, varies from platform to platform. For example, on PCs and Macs, there are menu-driven commands for opening, writing, editing, saving, and printing files whereas on UNIX machines, such as Sun Workstations, these tasks are usually performed with UNIX commands. Here's a brief list of the important platform-dependent features for PCs, Macs, and Unix machines.

- **Launching MATLAB :** If MATLAB is installed on your machine correctly then you can launch it by following these directions:

  On PCs and Macs: Navigate and find the MATLAB folder, locate the MATLAB program, and double-click on the program icon to launch MATLAB. If you have worked in MATLAB before and have an M-file or Mat-file that was written by MATLAB, you can also double-click on the file to launch MATLAB.

  On Unix machines: Type `matlab` on the Unix prompt and hit **return**. If MATLAB is somewhere in your *path*, it will be launched. If it is not, ask your system administrator.

- **Creating a directory and saving files:** Where should you save your files so that MATLAB can easily access them? Theoretically, you can create a directory/folder anywhere, save your files, and direct MATLAB to find those files. The most convenient place, however, to save all user-created files is in a directory (or folder) immediately below the directory (or folder) in which the MATLAB application program is installed (for PCs and Macs). This way all user-created files are automatically accessible to MATLAB. If you need to store the files somewhere else, you might have to specify the path to the files using the `path` command or change the working directory of MATLAB to the desired directory with the `cd` command. We recommend the latter.

  On PCs and Macs: Create a folder inside the MATLAB folder and save your files there. If you are not allowed to write in the MATLAB folder (as may be the case in some shared facilities), then create a folder where you are allowed (perhaps on your own floppy disk), copy the file `startup.m` from the **MATLAB/Toolbox/local** folder to your folder, and launch MATLAB by double-clicking on the `startup.m` file in your folder. This way MATLAB automatically accesses all files in your folder. You should also personalize the *Startup* file by editing it and adding a line, say, `disp('Hello Kelly, Welcome Aboard.')` You can open, write, and save M-files by selecting appropriate commands from the **File** menu in MATLAB.

  On Unix machines: Create a directory for your MATLAB work, save all MATLAB related files here, and launch MATLAB from this directory. To open, write, and save M-files, use a text editor such as **vi** or **emacs**.

- **Printing:**

  On PCs and Macs: To print the contents of the current active window (command, figure, or edit window), select **Print...** from the **File** menu and click **Print** in the dialog box. You can also print the contents of the figure window by typing `print` at the MATLAB prompt.

  On Unix machines: To print a file from inside MATLAB, type the appropriate Unix command preceded by the exclamation character (!). For example, to print the file **startup.m**, type `!lpr startup.m` on the MATLAB prompt. To print a graph that is currently in the figure window simply type `print` on the MATLAB prompt.

1.6.6   General commands you should remember

On-line help

help	lists topics on which help is available
help *topic*	provides help on *topic*
lookfor *string*	lists help topics containing *string*
expo	runs the demo program

Workspace information

who	lists variables currently in the workspace
whos	lists variables currently in the workspace with their size
what	lists m-, mat-, and mex-files on the disk
clear	clears the workspace, all variables are removed
clear x y z	clears only variables x, y and z

Directory information

pwd	shows the current working directory
cd	changes the current working directory
dir	lists contents of the current directory
ls	lists contents of the current directory, similar to dir

General information

computer	tells you the computer type you are using
clock	gives you wall clock time
date	tells you the date
more	controls the paged output according to the screen size
flops	tells you how many floating point operations you have used so far

Termination

^c (Control-c)	local abort, kills the current execution of a command or a program
quit	quits MATLAB
exit	same as quit

2. *Tutorial Lessons*

The following lessons are designed to get you started quickly in MATLAB. Each lesson should take about 10–15 minutes. The lessons are intended to make you familiar with the basic facilities of MATLAB. We urge you also to do the exercises given at the end of each lesson. This will take more time, but it will teach you quite a few things. If you get stuck in the exercises, simply turn the page; answers are on the back. Most answers consist of correct commands to do the exercises. But there are several correct ways of doing the problems. So, your commands might look different than those given.

Before You Start

You need some information about the computer you are going to work on. In particular, find out:

- How to switch on the computer and get it started.

- How to log on and log off.

- Where MATLAB is installed on the computer.

- How to access MATLAB.

- Where you can write and save files—hard drive or a floppy disk.

- If there a printer attached to the computer.

If you are working on your own computer, you will most likely know the answer to these questions. If you are working on a computer in a public facility, the system manager can help you. If you are in a class that requires working on MATLAB, your professor or TA can provide answers. In public facilities, sometimes the best thing to do is to spot a friendly person working there and ask these questions politely. People are usually nice!

If you have not read the introduction (Chapter 1), we recommend that you at least read Sections 1.6.1–1.6.3 and glance through the rest of Section 1.6 before trying the tutorials.

Here are the lessons in a nutshell:

Lesson-1: Log on, launch MATLAB, do some simple calculations, and quit.

> *Key features:* Learn to add, multiply, and exponentiate numbers, use trig functions, and control screen output with `format`.

Lesson-2: Create and work with arrays, vectors in particular.

> *Key features:* Learn to create, add, and multiply vectors, use `sin` and `sqrt` functions with vector arguments, and use `linspace` to create a vector.

Lesson-3: Plot simple graphs.

> *Key features:* Learn to plot, label, and print out a circle.

Lesson-4: Write and execute a *script file*.

> *Key features:* Learn to write, save, and execute a script file that plots a unit circle.

Lesson-5: Write and execute a *function files*. *Key features:* Learn to write, save, and execute a function file that plots a circle of any specified radius.

2.1   Lesson 1: A Minimum MATLAB Session

Goal: To learn how to log on, invoke MATLAB , do a few trivial calculations, quit MATLAB, and log off.

Time Estimates: *Lesson: 10 minutes,   Exercises: 30 minutes*

What you are going to learn:

- How to do simple arithmetic calculations. The arithmetic operators are:

+	addition,
−	subtraction,
*	multiplication,
/	division, and
^	exponentiation.

- How to assign values to variables.

- How to suppress screen output.

- How to control the appearance of floating point numbers on the screen.

- How to quit MATLAB.

The MATLAB commands/operators used are

```
+, -, *, /, ^, ;
sin, cos, log
format
quit
```

In addition, if you do the exercises, you will learn more about arithmetic operations, exponentiation and logarithms, trigonometric functions, and complex numbers.

Method: Log on and launch MATLAB. Once the MATLAB command window is on the screen, you are ready to carry out the first lesson. Some commands and their output are shown below. Go ahead and reproduce the results.

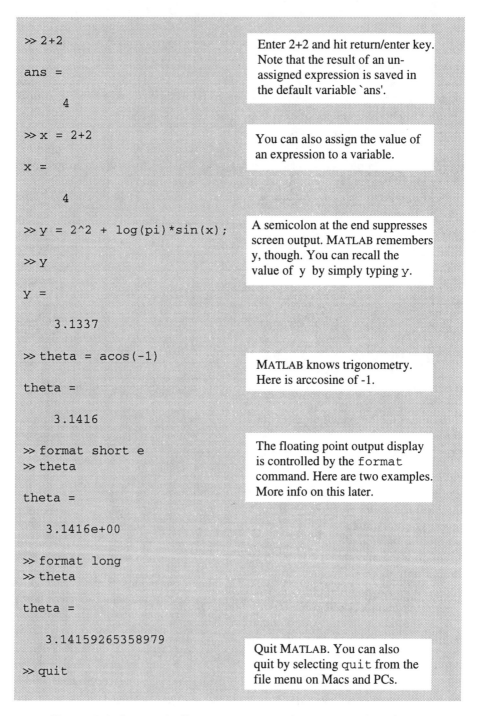

```
>> 2+2                          Enter 2+2 and hit return/enter key.
                                Note that the result of an un-
ans =                           assigned expression is saved in
                                the default variable `ans'.
     4

>> x = 2+2                      You can also assign the value of
                                an expression to a variable.
x =

     4

>> y = 2^2 + log(pi)*sin(x);    A semicolon at the end suppresses
                                screen output. MATLAB remembers
>> y                            y, though. You can recall the
                                value of y by simply typing y.
y =

     3.1337

>> theta = acos(-1)             MATLAB knows trigonometry.
                                Here is arccosine of -1.
theta =

     3.1416

>> format short e               The floating point output display
>> theta                        is controlled by the format
                                command. Here are two examples.
theta =                         More info on this later.

   3.1416e+00

>> format long
>> theta

theta =

   3.14159265358979
                                Quit MATLAB. You can also
                                quit by selecting quit from the
>> quit                         file menu on Macs and PCs.
```

Figure 2.1: Lesson-1: Some simple calculations in MATLAB.

EXERCISES

1. **Arithmetic operations:** Compute the following quantities:

   - $\frac{2^5}{2^5-1}$ and compare with $(1 - \frac{1}{2^5})^{-1}$.

   - $3\frac{\sqrt{5}-1}{(\sqrt{5}+1)^2} - 1$. The square root $\sqrt{x}$ can be calculated as `sqrt(x)` or `x^0.5`.

   - Area $= \pi r^2$ with $r = \pi^{\frac{1}{3}} - 1$. ($\pi$ is `pi` in MATLAB.)

2. **Exponential and logarithms:** The mathematical quantities e^x, $\ln x$, and $\log x$ are calculated with `exp(x)`, `log(x)`, and `log10(x)`, respectively. Calculate the following quantities:

   - e^3, $\ln(e^3)$, $\log_{10}(e^3)$, and $\log_{10}(10^5)$.

   - $e^{\pi\sqrt{163}}$.

   - Solve $3^x = 17$ for x and check the result. (The solution is $x = \frac{\ln 17}{\ln 3}$. You can verify the result by direct substitution.)

3. **Trigonometry:** The basic MATLAB trig functions are `sin`, `cos`, `tan`, `cot`, `sec`, and `csc`. The inverses, e.g., arcsin, arctan, etc., are calculated with `asin`, `atan`, etc. The same is true for hyperbolic functions. The inverse function `atan2` takes 2 arguments, `y` and `x`, and gives the four-quadrant inverse tangent. The argument of these functions must be in radians.

   Calculate the following quantities:

   - $\sin\frac{\pi}{6}$, $\cos\pi$, and $\tan\frac{\pi}{2}$.

   - $\sin^2\frac{\pi}{6} + \cos^2\frac{\pi}{6}$. (Typing `sin^2(x)` for $\sin^2 x$ will produce an error).

   - $y = \cosh^2 x - \sinh^2 x$, with $x = 32\pi$.

4. **Complex numbers:** MATLAB recognizes the letters i and j as the imaginary number $\sqrt{-1}$. A complex number $2 + 5i$ may be input as `2+5i` or `2+5*i` in MATLAB . The former case is always interpreted as a complex number whereas the latter case is taken as complex only if i has not been assigned any local value. The same is true for j. This kind of context dependence, for better or worse, pervades MATLAB.

   Compute the following quantities.

   - $\frac{1+3i}{1-3i}$. Can you check the result by hand calculation?

   - $e^{i\frac{\pi}{4}}$. Check the Euler's Formula $e^{ix} = \cos x + i\sin x$ by computing the right hand side, too.

   - Execute the commands `exp(pi/2*i)` and `exp(pi/2i)`. Can you explain the difference between the two results?

Answers to Exercises

---

1. | Command | Result |
   | --- | --- |
   | 2^5/(2^5-1) | 1.0323 |
   | 3*(sqrt(5)-1)/(sqrt(5)+1)^2 | 0.3541 |
   | area=pi*(pi^(1/3)-1)^2 | 0.6781 |

2. | Command | Result |
   | --- | --- |
   | exp(3) | 20.0855 |
   | log(exp(3)) | 3.0000 |
   | log10(exp(3)) | 1.3029 |
   | log10(10^5) | 5.0000 |
   | exp(pi*sqrt(163)) | 2.6254e+17 |
   | x=log(17)/log(3) | 2.5789 |

3. | Command | Result |
   | --- | --- |
   | sin(pi/6) | 0.5000 |
   | cos(pi) | -1.0000 |
   | tan(pi/2) | 1.6332e+16 (should be ∞.) |
   | (sin(pi/6))^2+(cos(pi/6))^2 | 1 |
   | x=32*pi; y=(cosh(x))^2-(sinh(x))^2 | 0 |

4. | Command | Result |
   | --- | --- |
   | (1+3i)/(1-3i) | -0.8000 + 0.6000i |
   | exp(i*pi/4) | 0.7071 + 0.7071i |
   | exp(pi/2*i) | 0.0000 + 1.0000i |
   | exp(pi/2i) | 0.0000 - 1.0000i |

   exp(pi/2*i)$= e^{\frac{\pi}{2}i} = \cos(\frac{\pi}{2}) + i\,\sin(\frac{\pi}{2})$

   exp(pi/2i)$= e^{\frac{\pi}{2i}} = e^{-\frac{\pi}{2}i} = \cos(\frac{\pi}{2}) - i\,\sin(\frac{\pi}{2})$

2.2 Lesson 2: Creating and Working with Arrays of Numbers

Goal: To learn how to create arrays and vectors, and how to perform arithmetic and trigonometric operations on them.

An *array* is a list of numbers or expressions arranged in horizontal rows and vertical columns. When an array has only one row or column, it is called a *vector*. An array with m rows and n columns is a called a *matrix* of size $m \times n$. See Section 3.1 for more information.

Time Estimates: *Lesson: 15 minutes,   Exercises: 45 minutes*

What you are going to learn:

- How to create row and column vectors.

- How to create a vector of n numbers linearly (equally) spaced between two given numbers a and b.

- How to do simple arithmetic operations on vectors.

- How to do *array operations*:

.*	term by term multiplication,
./	term by term division, and
.^	term by term exponentiation.

- How to use trigonometric functions with array arguments.

- How to use elementary math functions such as square root, exponentials, and logarithms, with array arguments.

This lesson deals with primarily one-dimensional arrays, i.e., vectors. One of the exercises introduces you to two-dimensional arrays, i.e., matrices. There are many mathematical concepts associated with vectors and matrices that we do not mention here. If you have some background in linear algebra, you will find that MATLAB is set up to do almost any matrix computation (e.g., inverse, determinant, rank, etc.).

Method: You already know how to launch MATLAB. So go ahead and try the commands shown on the next page. Once again, you are going to reproduce the results shown.

```
>> x = [1 2 3]

x =
     1     2     3

>> y = [2; 1; 5]

y =
     2
     1
     5

>> z = [2 1 0];
>> a = x + z

a =
     3     3     3

>> b = x + y

??? Error using ==> +
Matrix dimensions must agree.

>> a = x.*z

a =
     2     2     0

>> b = 2*a

b =
     4     4     0

>> x = linspace(0,10,5)

x =
         0    2.5000    5.0000    7.5000   10.0000

>> y = sin(x);

>> z = sqrt(x).*y

z =
         0    0.9463   -2.1442    2.5688   -1.7203
```

x is a row vector with 3 elements.

y is a column vector with 3 elements.

You can add (or subtract) two vectors of the same size.

But you cannot add (or subtract) a row vector to a column vector.

You can multiply (or divide) the elements of two same-sized vectors term by term with the *array operator* . * (or . /).

But multiplying a vector with a scalar does not need any special operation (no dot before the *).

Create a vector x with 5 elements **lin**early **spaced** between 0 and 10.

Trigonometric functions sin, cos, etc., as well as elementary math functions sqrt, exp, log, etc., operate on vectors term by term.

Figure 2.2: Lesson-2: Some simple calculations with vectors.

EXERCISES

1. **Equation of a straight line:** The equation of a straight line is $y = mx + c$ where m and c are constants. Compute the y-coordinates of a line with slope $m = 0.5$ and the intercept $c = -2$ at the following x-coordinates:

$$x = 0, \quad 1.5, \quad 3, \quad 4, \quad 5, \quad 7, \quad 9, \text{ and } 10.$$

   [Note: Your command should not involve any array operators since your calculation involves multiplication of a vector with a scalar m and then addition of another scalar c.]

2. **Multiply, divide, and exponentiate vectors:** Create a vector t with 10 elements: 1, 2, 3, ..., 10. Now compute the following quantities:

   - $x = t \sin(t)$.
   - $y = \frac{t-1}{t+1}$.
   - $z = \frac{\sin(t^2)}{t^2}$.

3. **Points on a circle:** All points with coordinates $x = r \cos \theta$ and $y = r \sin \theta$, where r is a constant, lie on a circle with radius r, i.e., they satisfy the equation $x^2 + y^2 = r^2$. Create a column vector for θ with the values 0, $\pi/4$, $\pi/2$, $3\pi/4$, π, and $5\pi/4$.

   Take $r = 2$ and compute the column vectors x and y. Now check that x and y indeed satisfy the equation of circle, by computing the radius $r = \sqrt{(x^2 + y^2)}$. [To calculate r you will need the array operator .^ for squaring x and y. Of course, you could compute x^2 by x.*x also.]

4. **The geometric series:** This is funky! You know how to compute x^n element-by-element for a vector x and a scalar exponent n. How about computing n^x, and what does it mean? The result is again a vector with elements n^{x_1}, n^{x_2}, n^{x_3} etc.

   The sum of a geometric series $1 + r + r^2 + r^3 + \ldots + r^n$ approaches the limit $\frac{1}{1-r}$ for $r < 1$ as $n \to \infty$. Create a vector n of 11 elements from 0 to 10. Take $r = 0.5$ and create another vector $x = [r^0 \quad r^1 \quad r^2 \quad \ldots \quad r^n]$ with the command x = r.^n . Now take the sum of this vector with the command s = sum(x) (s is the sum of the actual series). Calculate the limit $\frac{1}{1-r}$ and compare the computed sum s. Repeat the procedure taking n from 0 to 50 and then from 0 to 100.

5. **Matrices and vectors:** Go to Fig. 3.1 on page 44 and reproduce the results. Now create a vector and a matrix with the following commands: v = 0:0.2:12; and M = [sin(v); cos(v)];. Find the sizes of v and M using the **size** command. Extract the first 10 elements of each row of the matrix, and display them as column vectors.

Answers to Exercises

Commands to solve each problem are given below.

1. `x=[0 1.5 3 4 5 7 9 10];`

   `y = 0.5*x-2`

   [*Ans.* $y = [-2.0000 \quad -1.2500 \quad -0.5000 \; 0 \; 0.5000 \; 1.5000 \; 2.5000 \; 3.0000]$.]

2. `t=1:10;`

   `x = t.*sin(t)`

   `y = (t-1)./(t+1)`

   `z = sin(t.^2)./(t.^2)`

3. `theta = [0;pi/4;pi/2;3*pi/4;pi;5*pi/4]`

   `x=cos(theta); y=sin(theta);`

   `x.^2 + y.^2`

4. `n = 0:10;`

   `r = 0.5; x = r.^n;`

   `s1 = sum(x)`

   `n=0:50; x=r.^n; s2=sum(x)`

   `n=0:100; x=r.^n; s3=sum(x)`

   [*Ans.* $s1 = 1.9990$, $s2 = 2.0000$, and $s3 = 2$]

5. `v=0:0.2:12;`

   `M=[sin(v); cos(v)];`

   `size(v)`

   `size(M)`

   `M(:,1:10)'`

   [*Ans.* v is 1×61 and M is 2×61.

   The last command `M(:,1:10)'` picks out the first 10 elements from each row of M and transposes to give a 10×2 matrix.]

2.3   Lesson 3: Creating and Printing Simple Plots

Goal: To learn how to make a simple 2-D plot in MATLAB and print it out.

Time Estimates: *Lesson: 10 minutes,   Exercises: 40 minutes*

What you are going to learn:

- How to generate x and y coordinates of 100 equidistant points on a unit circle.

- How to plot x vs y and thus create the circle.

- How to set the scale of the x and y axes to be the same, so that the circle looks like a circle and not an ellipse.

- How to label the axes with text strings.

- How to title the graph with a text string.

- How to get a hardcopy of the graph.

The MATLAB commands used are `axis`, `xlabel`, `ylabel`, `title`, and `print`.

This lesson teaches you the most basic graphics commands. The exercises take you through various types of plots, overlay plots, and more involved graphics.

Method: You are going to draw a circle of unit radius. To do this, first generate the data (x- and y-coordinates of, say, 100 points on the circle), then plot the data, and finally print the graph. For generating data, use the parametric equation of a unit circle:

$$x = \cos\theta, \quad y = \sin\theta, \quad 0 \leq \theta \leq 2\pi.$$

In the sample session shown here, only the commands are shown. You should see the output on your screen.

`>>theta = linspace(0,2*pi,100);`	Create a linearly spaced 100 elements long vector `theta`.
`>>x = cos(theta);`	
`>>y = sin(theta);`	Calculate x and y coordinates.
`>>plot(x,y)`	Plot x vs. y. (see Section 6.1)
`>>axis('equal');`	Set the length scales of the two axes to be the same.
`>>xlabel('x')`	Label the x-axis with x.
`>>ylabel('y')`	Label the y-axis with y.
`>>title('Circle of unit radius')`	Put a title on the plot.
`>> print`	Print on the default printer.

Figure 2.3: Lesson-3: Plotting and printing a simple graph.

Comments:

- After you enter the command `plot(x,y)`, you should see an ellipse in the Figure Window. MATLAB draws an ellipse rather than a circle because of its default rectangular axes. The next command `axis('equal')`, directs MATLAB to use the same scale on both axes, so that a circle appears as a circle. You can also use `axis('square')` to override the default rectangular axes.

- The arguments of the `axis`, `xlabel`, `ylabel`, and `title` commands are text strings. Text strings are entered within single right-quote (') characters. For more information on text strings, see Section 3.2.6 on page 59.

- The `print` command sends the current plot to the printer connected your computer. If the default printer is a dot-matrix printer, the circle may not print as an exact circle. On the Macs, you can correct this problem by checking the **tall adjust** option in the print dialog box.

EXERCISES

1. **A simple sine plot:** Plot $y = \sin x$, $0 \le x \le 2\pi$, taking 100 linearly spaced points in the given interval. Label the axes and put 'Plot created by *yourname*' in the title.

2. **Line-styles:** Make the same plot as above, but rather than displaying the graph as a curve, show the unconnected data points. To display the data points with small circles, use `plot(x,y,'o')`. [Hint: You may peep into Section 5.1 on page 101 if you wish.] Now combine the two plots with the command `plot(x,y,x,y,'o')` to show the line through the data points as well as the distinct data points.

3. **An exponentially decaying sine plot:** Plot $y = e^{-0.4x} \sin x$, $0 \le x \le 4\pi$, taking 10, 50, and 100 points in the interval. [Be careful about computing y. You need array multiplication between `exp(-0.4*x)` and `sin(x)`. See Section 3.2.1 on page 52 for more discussion on array operations.]

4. **Space curve:** Use the command `plot3(x,y,z)` to plot the circular helix $x(t) = \sin t$, $y(t) = \cos t$, $z(t) = t$, $0 \le t \le 20$.

5. **On-line help:** Type `help plot` on the MATLAB prompt and hit return. If too much text flashes by the screen, type `more on`, hit return, and then type `help plot` again. This should give you paged screen output. Read through the on-line help. To move to the next page of the screen output, simply press the spacebar.

6. **Log scale plots:** The plot commands `semilogx`, `semilogy` and `loglog`, plot the x-values, the y-values, and both x- and y-values on a $\log_{10}$ scale, respectively.

   Create a vector `x = 0:10:1000`. Plot x vs. x^3 using the three log scale plot commands. [Hint: First, compute `y=x.^3` and then, use `semilogx(x,y)` etc.]

7. **Overlay plots:** Plot $y = \cos x$ and $z = 1 - \frac{x^2}{2} + \frac{x^4}{24}$ for $0 \le x \le \pi$ on the same plot. You might like to read Section 5.1.4 on page 105 to learn how to plot multiple curves on the same graph. [Hint: You can use `plot(x,y,x,z,'--')` or you can plot the first curve, use the `hold on` command, and then plot the second curve on top of the first one.]

8. **Fancy plots:** Go to Section 5.1.5 on page 109 and look at the examples of specialized 2D plots on pages 110–113. Reproduce any of the plots you like.

9. **A very difficult plot:** Use your knowledge of *splines* and *interpolation* to draw a lizard (just kidding).

Answers to Exercises

Commands required to solve the problems are shown below.

1. ```
x=linspace(0,2*pi,100);
plot(x,sin(x))
xlabel('x'), ylabel('sin(x)')
title('Plot created by Rudra Pratap')
```

2. ```
plot(x,sin(x),x,sin(x),'o')
xlabel('x'), ylabel('sin(x)')
```

3. ```
x=linspace(0,4*pi,10);   % with 10 points
y=exp(-.4*x).*sin(x);
plot(x,y)
x=linspace(0,4*pi,50);   % with 50 points
y=exp(-.4*x).*sin(x);
plot(x,y)
x=linspace(0,4*pi,100); % with 100 points
y=exp(-.4*x).*sin(x);
plot(x,y)
```

4. ```
t=linspace(0,20,100);
plot3(sin(t),cos(t),t)
```

5. You should not be looking for answer here.

6. ```
x=0:10:1000;
y=x.^3;
semilogx(x,y)
semilogy(x,y)
loglog(x,y)
```

7. ```
x=linspace(0,pi,100);
y=cos(x); z=1-x.^2/2+x.^4/24;
plot(x,y,x,z)
plot(x,y,x,z,'--')
legend('cos(x)','z')    % try this legend command
```

[For fun: If the last command **legend** does produce a legend on your plot, click and hold your mouse on the legend and see if you can move it to a location of your liking. See page 103 for more information on **legend**.]

2.4 Lesson 4: Creating, Saving, and Executing a Script File

Goal: To learn how to create Script files and execute them in MATLAB.

A *Script File* is a user-created file with a sequence of MATLAB commands in it. The file must be saved with a '.m' extension to its name, thereby, making it an *M-file*. A script file is executed by typing its name (without the '.m' extension') at the command prompt. For more information, see Section 4.1 on page 73.

Time Estimates: *Lesson: 20 minutes,   Exercises: 30 minutes*

What you are going to learn:

- How to create, write, and save a script file.

- How to execute the script file in MATLAB.

Unfortunately, creating, editing, and saving files are highly system dependent tasks. The commands needed to accomplish these tasks depends on the operating system and the text editor you use. It is not possible to provide an introduction to these topics here. So, we assume that

- You know how to use a text editor on your Unix system (for example, **vi** or **emacs**), or that you're using the built-in MATLAB editor on a Mac or a PC.

- You know how to open, edit, and save a file.

- You know which directory your file is saved in.

Method: Write a script file to draw the unit circle of Lesson-3. You are essentially going to write the commands shown in Fig. 2.3 in a file, save it, name it, and execute it in MATLAB. Follow the directions below.

1. Create a new file:

    - **On PC's and Macs:** Select **New M-File** from the **File** menu. A new edit window should appear.

    - **On Unix workstations:** Type !vi circle.m or !emacs circle.m at the MATLAB prompt to open an edit window in **vi** or **emacs**.

2. Type the following lines into this file. Lines starting with a % sign are interpreted as comment lines by MATLAB and are ignored.

```
% CIRCLE - A script file to draw a unit circle
% File written by Rudra Pratap. Last modified 9/14/94

theta = linspace(0,2*pi,100);      % create vector theta
x = cos(theta);                    % generate x-coordinates
y = sin(theta);                    % generate y-coordinates
plot(x,y);                         % plot the circle
axis('equal');                     % set equal scale on axes
title('Circle of unit radius')     % put a title
```

3. Write and save the file under the name **circle.m**:

   - **On PC's and Macs:** Select **Save As...** from the **File** menu. A dialog box should appear. Type the name of the document as `circle.m`. Make sure the file is being saved in the folder you want it to be in (the current working folder/directory of MATLAB). Click **Save** to save the file.

   - **On Unix workstations:** You are on your own to write and save the file using the editor of your choice. After writing the file, quit the editor to get back to MATLAB.

4. Now get back to MATLAB and type the following commands in the command window to execute the script file.

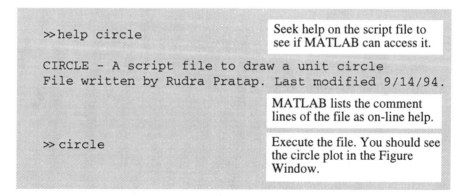

Figure 2.4: Lesson-4: Executing a script file.

EXERCISES

1. **Show the center of the circle:** Modify the script file `circle` to show the center of the circle on the plot, too. Show the center point with a '+'. (Hint: See Exercises 2 and 7 of Lesson 3.)

2. **Change the radius of the circle:** Modify the script file `circle.m` to draw a circle of arbitrary radius r as follows:

   - Include the following command in the script file before the first executable line (`theta = ...`) to ask the user to input (r) on the screen:
     $$r = \text{input('Enter the radius of the circle: ')}$$
   - Modify the x and y coordinate calculations appropriately.
   - Save and execute the file. When asked, enter a value for the radius and press return.

3. **Variables in the workspace:** All variables created by a script file are left in the global workspace. You can get information about them and access them, too:

   - Type `who` to see the variables present in your workspace. You should see the variables `theta, x` and `y` in the list.
   - Type `whos` to get more information about the variables and the workspace.
   - Type `[theta' x' y']` to see the values of θ, x and y listed as three columns. All three variables are row vectors. Typing a single right quote (`'` on the keyboard) after their name transposes them and makes them column vectors.

4. **Contents of the file:** You can see the contents of an M-file without opening the file with an editor. The contents are displayed by the `type` command. To see the contents of `circle.m`, type `type circle.m`.

5. **H1 line:** The first commented line before any executable statement in a script file is called the *H1 line*. It is this line that is searched by the `lookfor` command. Since the `lookfor` command is used to look for M-files with keywords in their description, you should put keywords in H1 line of all M-files you create. Type `lookfor unit` to see what MATLAB comes up with. Does it list the script file you just created?

6. **Just for fun:** Write a script file that, when executed, greets you, displays the date and time, and curses your favorite TA or professor. [The commands you need are `disp, date, clock`, and possibly `fix`. See on-line help on these commands before using them.]

Answers to Exercises

1. Replace the command plot(x,y) by the command plot(x,y,0,0,'+').

2. Your changed script file should look like this:

```
% CIRCLE - A script file to draw a unit circle
% File written by Rudra Pratap on 9/14/94. Last modified 6/15/95

r = input('Enter the radius of the circle: ')
theta = linspace(0,2*pi,100);      % create vector theta
x = r*cos(theta);                  % generate x-coordinates
y = r*sin(theta);                  % generate y-coordinates
plot(x,y);                         % plot the circle
axis('equal');                     % set equal scale on axes
title('Circle of given radius r')   % put a title
```

6. Here is a script file that you may not fully understand yet. Do not worry, just copy it if you like it. See on-line help on the commands used, e.g. disp, date, fix, clock, int2str.

```
% Script file to begin your day. Save it as Hi_there.m
% To execute, just type Hi_there
% File written by Rudra Pratap on 6/15/95.
% -------------------------------
disp('Hello R.P., How is life?')
disp(' ')                          % display a blank line
disp('Today is...')
disp(date)                         % display date
time=fix(clock);                   % get time as integers
hourstr=int2str(time(4));          % get the hour
minstr=int2str(time(5));           % get the minute
if time(5)<10                      % if minute is, say 5, then
    minstr=['0',minstr];           %- write it as 05.
end
timex = [hourstr ':' minstr  merid]; % create the time string
disp(' ')
disp('And the time is..')
disp(timex)                        % display the time
```

2.5   Lesson 5: Creating and Executing a Function File

Goal: To learn how to write and execute a *function file*. Also, to learn the difference between a script file and a function file.

A *function file* is also an M-file, just like a script file, except it has a function definition line on the top that defines the input and output explicitly. For more information, see Section 4.2.

Time Estimates: *Lesson: 15 minutes,   Exercises: 60 minutes*

What you are going to learn:

- How to open and edit an existing M-file.

- How to define and execute a function file.

Method: Write a function file to draw a circle of a specified radius, with the radius as the input to the function. You can either write the function file from scratch or modify the script file of Lesson 4. We advise you to select the latter option.

1. Open the script file **circle.m**:

   - **On PC's and Macs:** Select **Open M-File** from the **File** menu. Navigate and select the file **circle.m** from the **Open** dialog box. Double click to open the file. The contents of the file should appear in an edit window.

   - **On Unix workstations:** Type !vi circle.m or !emacs circle.m on the MATLAB prompt to open the file in a **vi** or **emacs** window.

2. Edit the file **circle.m** to look like the following.

```
function [x,y] = circlefn(r);
% CIRCLEFN - Function to draw a circle of radius r.
% File written by Rudra Pratap on 9/17/94. Last modified 9/17/94
% Call syntax:   [x,y] = circlefn(r);  or just:  circlefn(r);
% Input:      r = specified radius
% Output: [x,y] = the x- and y-coordinates of data points
theta = linspace(0,2*pi,100);  % create vector theta
x = r*cos(theta);              % generate x-coordinates
y = r*sin(theta);              % generate y-coordinates
plot(x,y);                     % plot the circle
axis('equal');                 % set equal scale on axes
title(['Circle of radius r =',num2str(r)])
                               % put a title with the value of r.
```

3. Now write and save the file under the name **circlefn.m** as follows:

- **On PC's and Macs:** Select **Save As...** from the **File** menu. A dialog box should appear. Type the name of the document as `circlefn.m` (usually, MATLAB automatically writes the name of the function in the document name). Make sure the file is saved in the folder you want (the current working folder/directory of MATLAB). Click **save** to save the file.

- **On Unix workstations:** You are on your own to write and save the file using the editor of your choice. After writing the file, quit the editor to get back to MATLAB.

4. Here is a sample session that executes the function **circlefn** in three different ways. Try it out.

```
>> R = 5;
>> [x,y] = circlefn(R);
```
Specify the input and execute the function with an explicit output list.

```
>> [cx,cy] = circlefn(2.5);
```
You can also specify the value of the input directly.

```
>> circlefn(1);
```
If you don't need the output, you don't have to specify it.

```
>> circlefn(R^2/(R+5*sin(R)));
```
Of course, the input can also be a valid MATLAB expression.

Figure 2.5: Lesson-5: Executing a function file.

Comments:

- Note that a function file (see previous page) must begin with a function definition line. To learn more about function files, refer to Section 4.2 on page 76.

- The argument of the `title` command in this function file is slightly complicated. To understand how it works see Section 3.2.6 on page 59.

EXERCISES

1. **On-line help:** Type `help function` to get on-line help on `function`. Read through the help file.

2. **Convert temperature:** Write a function that outputs a conversion-table for Celsius and Fahrenheit temperatures. The input of the function should be two numbers: T_i and T_f, specifying the lower and upper range of the table in Celsius. The output should be a two column matrix: the first column showing the temperature in Celsius from T_i to T_f in the increments of 1°C and the second column showing the corresponding temperatures in Fahrenheit. To do this, (i) create a column vector C from T_i to T_f with the command `C = [Ti:Tf]'`, (ii) calculate the corresponding numbers in Fahrenheit using the formula $[F = \frac{9}{5}C + 32]$, and (iii) make the final matrix with the command `temp = [C F];`. Note that your output will be named `temp`.

3. **Calculate factorials:** Write a function `factorial` to compute the factorial $n!$ for any integer n. The input should be the number n and the output should be $n!$. You might have to use a *for* loop or a *while* loop to do the calculation. See Section 4.4.4, page 92 for a quick description of these loops. (You can use the built-in function `prod` to calculate factorials. For example, $n! = $`prod(1:n)`. In this exercise, however, do not use this function.)

4. **Compute the cross product:** Write a function file `crossprod` to compute the cross product of two vectors **u**, and **v**, given $\mathbf{u} = (u_1, u_2, u_3)$, $\mathbf{v} = (v_1, v_2, v_3)$, and $\mathbf{u} \times \mathbf{v} = (u_2 v_3 - u_3 v_2, u_3 v_1 - u_1 v_3, u_1 v_2 - u_2 v_1)$. Check your function by taking cross products of pairs of unit vectors: $(\mathbf{i}, \mathbf{j})$, $(\mathbf{j}, \mathbf{k})$, etc. $[\mathbf{i} = (1, 0, 0), \mathbf{j} = (0, 1, 0), \mathbf{k} = (0, 0, 1)]$. (Do not use the built-in function `cross` here.)

5. **Sum a geometric series:** Write a function to compute the sum of a geometric series $1 + r + r^2 + r^3 + \ldots + r^n$ for a given r and n. Thus the input to the function must be r and n and the output must be the sum of the series. [See Exercise 4 of Lesson 2.]

6. **Calculate the interest on your money:** The interest you get at the end of n years, at a flat annual rate of $r\%$, depends on how the interest is compounded. If the interest is added to your account k times a year, and the principal amount you invested is X_0, then at the end of n years you would have $X = X_0 \left(1 + \frac{r}{k}\right)^{kn}$ amount of money in your account. Write a function to compute the interest $(X - X_0)$ on your account for a given X, n, r, and k.

   Use the function to find the difference between the interest paid on $1000 at the rate of 6% a year at the end of 5 years if the interest is compounded (i) quarterly ($k = 4$) and (ii) daily ($k = 365$).

Answers to Exercises

Some of the commands in the following functions might be too advanced for you at this point. If so, look them up or ignore them.

2.
```
function temptable = ctof(tinitial,tfinal);
% CTOF : function to convert temperature from C to F
% call syntax:
%           temptable = ctof(tinitial,tfinal);
% ------------
C = [tinitial:tfinal]';      % create a column vector C
F = (9/5)*C + 32;            % compute corresponding F
temptable = [C F];           % make a 2 column matrix of C & F.
```

3.
```
function factn = factorial(n);
% FACTORIAL: function to compute factorial n!
% call syntax:
%           factn = factorial(n);
% ------------
factn = 1;                   % initialize. also 0! = 1.
for k = n:-1:1               % go from n to 1
    factn = factn*k;         % multiply n by n-1, n-2 etc.
end
```

4.
```
function w = crossprod(u,v);
% CROSSPROD: function to compute w = u x v for vectors u & v.
% call syntax:
%           w = crossprod(u,v);
% ------------
if length(u)>3 | length(v)>3  % check if u OR v has more than 3 elements
    error('Ask Euler. This cross product is beyond me.')
end
w = [u(2)*v(3)-u(3)*v(2);     % first element of w
     u(3)*v(1)-u(1)*v(3);     % second element of w
     u(1)*v(2)-u(2)*v(1)];    % third element of w
```

```
5. function s = gseriessum(r,n);
   % GSERIESSUM: function to calculate the sum of a geometric series
   % The series is  1+r+r^2+r^3+....r^n (upto nth power).
   % call syntax:
   %           s = gseriessum(r,n);
   % ------------
   nvector = 0:n;                   % create a vector from 0 to n
   series = r.^nvector;             % create a vector of terms in the series
   s = sum(series);                 % sum all elements of the vector 'series'.
```

```
6. function [capital,interest] = compound(capital,years,rate,timescomp);
   % COMPOUND: function to compute the compounded capital and the interest
   % call syntax:
   %           [capital,interest] = compound(capital,years,rate,timescomp);
   % ------------
   x0 = capital; n = years; r = rate; k = timescomp;
   if r>1                           % check for common mistake
      disp('check your interest rate. For 8% enter .08, not 8.')
   end
   capital = x0*(1+r/k)^(k*n);
   interest = capital - x0;
```

[*Ans.* (i) Quarterly: $346.85,   Daily: $349.83,   Difference: $ 3.02.]

3. *Interactive Computation*

In principle, one can do all calculations in MATLAB interactively, by entering commands sequentially in the command window, although a *script file* (explained in Section 4.1) is perhaps a better choice for computations that involve more than a few steps. The interactive mode of computation, however, makes MATLAB a powerful scientific calculator that puts hundreds of built-in mathematical functions for numerical calculations and sophisticated graphics at the finger tips of the user.

In this chapter, we introduce you to some of MATLAB's built-in functions and capabilities, through examples of interactive computation. The basic things to keep in mind are:

Where to type commands: All MATLAB commands or expressions are entered in the command window at the MATLAB prompt '≫ '.

How to execute commands: To execute a command or statement, you must press return or enter at the end.

What to do if the command is very long: If your command does not fit on one line you can continue the command on the next line if you type three consecutive periods at the end of the first line. You can keep continuing this way till the length of your command hits the limit, which is 4096 characters. For more information see the discussion on **Continuation** on pages 42 and 90.

How to name variables: Names of variables must begin with a letter. After the first letter, any number of digits or underscores may be used, but MATLAB remembers only the first 19 characters.

What is the precision of computation: All computations are carried out internally in double precision. The appearance of numbers on the screen, however, depends on the `format` in use (see Section 1.6.3).

How to control the display format of output: The output appearance of floating point numbers (number of digits after the decimal etc.) is controlled with the `format` command. The default is `format short`, which displays four digits after the decimal. For other available formats and how to change them, see Section 1.6.3 or on-line help on `format` .

How to suppress the screen output: A semicolon (;) at the end of a command suppresses the screen output, although the command is carried out and the result is saved in the variable assigned to the command or in the default variable `ans`.

How to set paged-screen display: For paged-screen display (one screenful of output display at a time) use the command `more on`.

Where and how to save results: If you need to save some of the computed results for later processing, you can save the variables in a file in binary or ASCII format with the `save` command. See Section 3.4 on page 68 for more information.

How to print your work: You can print your entire session in MATLAB, part of it, or selected segments of it, in one of several various ways. The simplest way, perhaps, is to create a diary with the `diary` command (see Section 3.4.2 for more information) and save your entire session in it. Then you can print the diary just the way you would print any other file on your computer. On PCs and Macs, however, you can print the session by selecting **Print** from the **File** menu. (Before you print, make sure that the command window is the active window. If it isn't, just click on the command window to make it active).

What about comments: MATLAB takes anything following a % as a comment and ignores it. [1] You are not likely to use a lot of comments while computing interactively, but you will use them when you write programs in MATLAB.

---

[1] except when the % appears in a quote enclosed character string or in certain I/O format statements.

Since MATLAB derives most of its power from matrix computations and assumes every variable to be, at least potentially, a matrix, we start with descriptions and examples of how to enter, index, manipulate, and perform some useful calculations with matrices.

3.1 Matrices and Vectors

3.1.1 Input

[1] *On-line help category:* `elmat`

A matrix is entered row-wise, with consecutive elements of a row separated by a space or a comma, and the rows separated by semicolons or carriage returns. The entire matrix must be enclosed within square brackets. Elements of the matrix may be real numbers, complex numbers, or valid MATLAB expressions.

Examples:

Matrix	**MATLAB input command**
$A = \begin{bmatrix} 1 & 2 & 5 \\ 3 & 9 & 0 \end{bmatrix}$	`A = [1 2 5; 3 9 0]`
$B = \begin{bmatrix} 2x & \ln x + \sin y \\ 5i & 3 + 2i \end{bmatrix}$	`B = [2*x log(x)+sin(y); 5i 3+2i]`

Special cases: vectors and scalars

- A vector is a special case of a matrix, with just one row or one column. It is entered the same way as a matrix.

  Examples: u = [1 3 9] produces a row vector,

  v = [1; 3; 9] produces a column vector.

- A scalar does not need brackets.

  Example: g = 9.81;

- Square brackets with no elements between them create a null matrix.

  Example: X = []. (See Fig. 3.1 for a more useful example).

---

[1]This box lets you know that you can learn more about this topic from MATLAB's online help, in the help category called *elmat* (for *el*ementary *mat*rix manipulations).

Continuation

If it is not possible to type the entire input on the same line then use three consecutive periods (...) to signal continuation, and continue the input on the next line. The three periods are called an *ellipsis*. For example,

```
A = [1/3    5.55*sin(x)   9.35   0.097;...
       3/(x+2*log(x))   3    0    6.555; ...
       (5*x-23)/55    x-3    x*sin(x)    sqrt(3)];
```

produces the intended 3×4 matrix A (provided, of course, x has been assigned a value before). A matrix can also be entered across multiple lines using carriage returns at the end of each row. In this case, the semicolons and ellipses at the end of each row may be omitted. Thus, the following three commands are equivalent:

```
A = [1 3 9; 5 10 15; 0 0 -5];
A = [1 3 9
       5 10 15
       0 0 -5];
A = [1 3 9; 5 10 ...
       15; 0 0 -5];
```

Continuation across several input lines achieved through '...' is not limited to matrix input. This construct may be used for other commands and for a long list of command arguments (see Section 4.4.2), as long as the command does not exceed 4096 characters.

3.1.2   Indexing (or Subscripting)

Once a matrix exists, its elements are accessed by specifying their row and column indices. Thus A(i,j) in MATLAB refers to the element a_{ij} of matrix A, i.e. the element in the ith row and jth column. This notation is fairly common in computational software packages and programming languages. MATLAB, however, provides a much higher level of index specification — it allows a range of rows and columns to be specified at the same time. For example, the statement A(m:n,k:l) specifies rows m to n and columns k to l of matrix A. When the rows (or columns) to be specified range over all rows (or columns) of the matrix, a colon can be used as the row (or column) index. Thus A(:,5:20) refers to the elements in columns 5 through 20 of *all* the rows of matrix A. This feature makes matrix manipulation much easier and provides a way to take advantage of the 'vectorized' nature of calculations in MATLAB. (See Fig. 3.1 for examples).

Dimension

Matrix dimensions are determined automatically by MATLAB, i.e., no explicit dimension declarations are required. The dimensions of an existing matrix A may be obtained with the command `size(A)` or more explicitly with `[m,n] = size(A)`,, which assigns the number of rows and columns of A to the variables m and n. When a matrix is entered by specifying a single element or a few elements of the matrix, MATLAB creates a matrix just big enough to accommodate the elements. Thus if the matrices B and C do not exist already, then

$$ \texttt{B(2,3) = 5;} \qquad \text{produces} \qquad B = \begin{bmatrix} 0 & 0 & 0 \\ 0 & 0 & 5 \end{bmatrix}, $$

$$ \texttt{C(3,1:3) = [1 2 3];} \quad \text{produces} \qquad C = \begin{bmatrix} 0 & 0 & 0 \\ 0 & 0 & 0 \\ 1 & 2 & 3 \end{bmatrix}. $$

3.1.3 Matrix Manipulation

As you can see from examples in Fig. 3.1, it is fairly easy to correct wrong entries of a matrix, extract any part or submatrix of a matrix, or delete or add rows and columns. These manipulations are done with MATLAB's smart indexing feature. By specifying vectors as the row and column indices of a matrix one can reference and modify any submatrix of a matrix. Thus if A is a 10×10 matrix, B is a 5×10 matrix, and y is a 20 elements long row vector, then `A([1 3 6 9],:) = [B(1:3,:); y(1:10)]` replaces 1st, 3rd, and 6th rows of A by the first 3 rows of B, and the 9th row of A by the first 10 elements of y. In such manipulations, it is imperative, of course, that the sizes of the submatrices to be manipulated are compatible. For example, in the above assignment, number of columns in A and B must be the same, and the total number of rows input on the right hand side must be the same as the number of rows specified on the left.

A more sophisticated use of the indexing with vectors is to use 0-1 vectors (usually created by relational operations) to reference submatrices. For example, let `v = [1 0 0 1 1]` and Q be a 5×5 matrix. Then `Q(v,:)` picks out those rows of Q where v is non-zero, i.e., the 1st, 4th, and 5th rows:

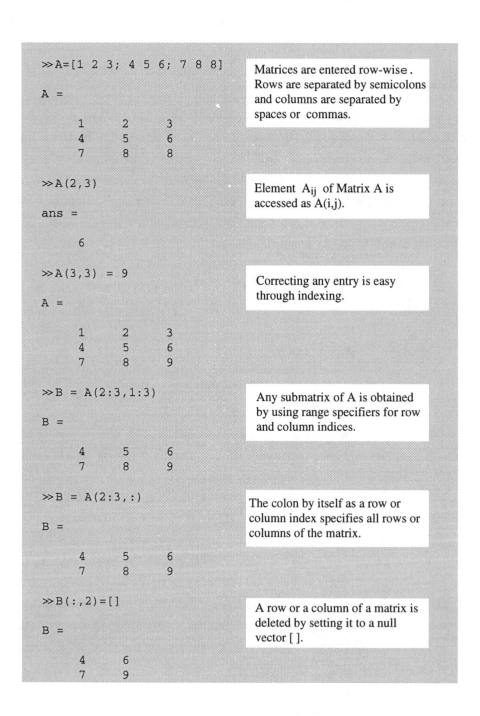

Figure 3.1: Examples of matrix input and matrix index manipulation.

$$\text{So, if} \quad Q = \begin{bmatrix} 2 & 3 & 6 & 0 & 5 \\ 0 & 0 & 20 & -4 & 3 \\ 1 & 2 & 3 & 9 & 8 \\ 2 & -5 & 5 & -5 & 6 \\ 5 & 10 & 15 & 20 & 25 \end{bmatrix} \quad \text{and} \quad v = \begin{bmatrix} 1 & 0 & 0 & 1 & 1 \end{bmatrix},$$

$$\text{then,} \quad \texttt{Q(v,:)} = \begin{bmatrix} 2 & 3 & 6 & 0 & 5 \\ 2 & -5 & 5 & -5 & 6 \\ 5 & 10 & 15 & 20 & 25 \end{bmatrix}.$$

Warning: Manipulating a matrix with 0-1 vectors, as shown in the example above, requires the 0-1 vector to have the same length as the range of the index that is being manipulated, e.g., if the vector is used as the row index then it must have the same length as the number of rows in the matrix. Thus, in the example above, the length of v must be 5 (equal to the number of rows of Q). What if v has different length? Well, then elements of v will be interpreted simply as the row indices of Q, and *not* as the elements of a *logical* vector. Consequently, a zero as an element of v, in this case, will cause an error (a zero is not allowed as a row or column index). Thus, if u=[1 1] and v=[1 1 0 0 0], then Q(u,:) and Q(v,:) produce very different matrices! Can you guess the results? If not, try it out in MATLAB. This is one example of a confusion that MATLAB creates when it tries to be cute and clever.

Matrices can also be reshaped. For example, all the elements of a matrix A can be strung into a single column vector b by the command b = A(:) (matrix A is stacked in vector b columnwise). It is also possible to reshape matrices to any size, using the **reshape** command (see on-line help).

Now let us look at some frequently used manipulations.

Transpose

The transpose of a matrix A is obtained by typing A', i.e., the name of the matrix followed by the single right quote. For a real matrix A, the command B = A' produces $B = A^T$, that is, $b_{ij} = a_{ji}$, and for a complex matrix A, B = A' produces the conjugate transpose $B = \bar{A}^T$, that is, $b_{ij} = \bar{a}_{ji}$.

Examples:

If $A = \begin{bmatrix} 2 & 3 \\ 6 & 7 \end{bmatrix}$,   then B = A' gives $B = \begin{bmatrix} 2 & 6 \\ 3 & 7 \end{bmatrix}$.

If $C = \begin{bmatrix} 2 & 3+i \\ 6i & 7i \end{bmatrix}$,   then Ct = C' gives $Ct = \begin{bmatrix} 2 & -6i \\ 3-i & -7i \end{bmatrix}$.

If $u = [0\ 1\ 2\ \cdots\ 9]$,   then v = u(3:6)' gives $v = \begin{bmatrix} 2 \\ 3 \\ 4 \\ 5 \end{bmatrix}$.

Initialization

Initialization of a matrix is not necessary in MATLAB. However, it is advisable in the following two cases.

1. **Large matrices:** If you are going to generate or manipulate a large matrix, initialize the matrix to a zero matrix of the required dimension. An $m \times n$ matrix can be initialized by the command A = zeros(m,n). The initialization reserves for the matrix a contiguous block in the computer's memory. Matrix operations performed on such matrices are generally more efficient.

2. **Dynamic matrices:** If the rows or columns of a matrix are computed in a loop (e.g. for or while loop) and appended to the matrix (see below) in each execution of the loop, then you might want to initialize the matrix to a null matrix before the loop starts. A null matrix A is created by the command A = []. Once created, a row or column of any size may be appended to A as described below.

Appending a row or column

A row can be easily appended to an existing matrix provided the row has the same length as the length of the rows of the existing matrix. The same thing goes for columns. The command A = [A u] appends the column vector u to the columns of A, while A = [A; v] appends the row vector v to the rows of A. A row or column of any size may be appended to a null matrix.

Examples: If

$$A = \begin{bmatrix} 1 & 0 & 0 \\ 0 & 1 & 0 \\ 0 & 0 & 1 \end{bmatrix}, \quad u = \begin{bmatrix} 5 & 6 & 7 \end{bmatrix}, \text{ and } v = \begin{bmatrix} 2 \\ 3 \\ 4 \end{bmatrix},$$

then

A = [A; u]   produces $A = \begin{bmatrix} 1 & 0 & 0 \\ 0 & 1 & 0 \\ 0 & 0 & 1 \\ 5 & 6 & 7 \end{bmatrix}$,   a 4 × 3 matrix,

A = [A v]   produces $A = \begin{bmatrix} 1 & 0 & 0 & 2 \\ 0 & 1 & 0 & 3 \\ 0 & 0 & 1 & 4 \end{bmatrix}$,   a 3 × 4 matrix,

A = [A u']   produces $A = \begin{bmatrix} 1 & 0 & 0 & 5 \\ 0 & 1 & 0 & 6 \\ 0 & 0 & 1 & 7 \end{bmatrix}$,   a 3 × 4 matrix,

A = [A u]   produces   an error,

B = []; B = [B; 1 2 3]   produces $B = \begin{bmatrix} 1 & 2 & 3 \end{bmatrix}$, and

B=[]; for k=1:3, B=[B; k k+1 k+2]; end   produces $B = \begin{bmatrix} 1 & 2 & 3 \\ 2 & 3 & 4 \\ 3 & 4 & 5 \end{bmatrix}$.

Deleting a row or column

Any row(s) or column(s) of a matrix can be deleted by setting the row or column to a null vector.

Examples:

A(2,:)   = []   deletes the 2nd row of matrix A,
A(:,3:5) = []   deletes the 3rd through 5th columns of A,
A([1 3],:) = []   deletes the 1st and the 3rd row of A,
u(5:length(u)) = []   deletes all elements of vector u except 1 through 4.

On-line
help
category:
elmat

Utility matrices

To aid to matrix generation and manipulation, MATLAB provides many useful utility matrices. For example,

eye(m,n)	returns an m by n matrix with 1's on the main diagonal
zeros(m,n)	returns an m by n matrix of zeros
ones(m,n)	returns an m by n matrix of ones
rand(m,n)	returns an m by n matrix of random numbers
randn(m,n)	returns an m by n matrix of normally distributed random numbers
diag(v)	generates a diagonal matrix with vector v on the diagonal
diag(A)	extracts the diagonal of matrix A as a vector
diag(A,1)	extracts the first upper off-diagonal vector of matrix A.

The first four commands with a single argument, e.g. ones(m), produce square matrices of dimension m. For example, eye(3) produces a 3×3 identity matrix. A matrix can be built with many block matrices as well. See examples in Fig. 3.2.

Here is a list of some more functions used in matrix manipulation:

rot90	rotates a matrix by 90°
fliplr	flips a matrix matrix from left to right
flipud	flips a matrix matrix from up to down
tril	extracts the lower triangular part of a matrix
triu	extracts the upper triangular part of a matrix
reshape	changes the shape of a matrix.

On-line
help
category:
specmat

Special matrices

There is also a set of built-in special matrices such as hadamard, hankel, hilb, invhilb, kron, pascal, toeplitz, vander, magic, etc. For a complete list and help on these matrices, type help specmat.

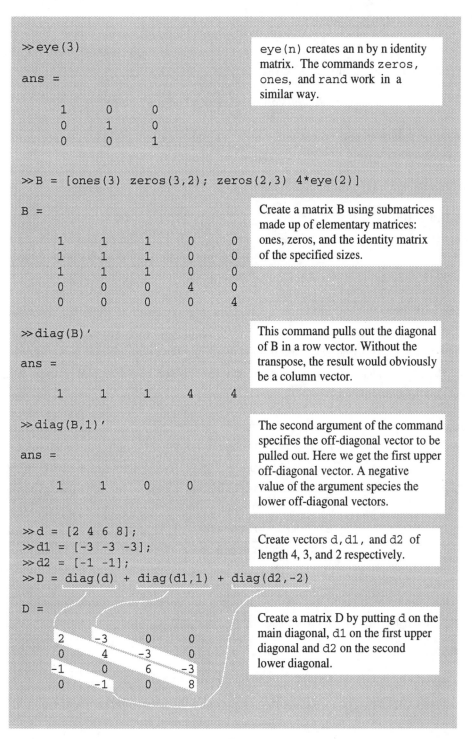

```
>> eye(3)

ans =

     1     0     0
     0     1     0
     0     0     1
```

eye(n) creates an n by n identity matrix. The commands zeros, ones, and rand work in a similar way.

```
>> B = [ones(3) zeros(3,2); zeros(2,3) 4*eye(2)]

B =

     1     1     1     0     0
     1     1     1     0     0
     1     1     1     0     0
     0     0     0     4     0
     0     0     0     0     4
```

Create a matrix B using submatrices made up of elementary matrices: ones, zeros, and the identity matrix of the specified sizes.

```
>> diag(B)'

ans =

     1     1     1     4     4
```

This command pulls out the diagonal of B in a row vector. Without the transpose, the result would obviously be a column vector.

```
>> diag(B,1)'

ans =

     1     1     0     0
```

The second argument of the command specifies the off-diagonal vector to be pulled out. Here we get the first upper off-diagonal vector. A negative value of the argument species the lower off-diagonal vectors.

```
>> d = [2 4 6 8];
>> d1 = [-3 -3 -3];
>> d2 = [-1 -1];
>> D = diag(d) + diag(d1,1) + diag(d2,-2)
```

Create vectors d, d1, and d2 of length 4, 3, and 2 respectively.

```
D =

     2    -3     0     0
     0     4    -3     0
    -1     0     6    -3
     0    -1     0     8
```

Create a matrix D by putting d on the main diagonal, d1 on the first upper diagonal and d2 on the second lower diagonal.

Figure 3.2: Examples of matrix manipulation using utility matrices and functions.

3.1.4   Creating Vectors

Very often we need to create a vector of numbers over a given range with a specified increment. The general command to do this in MATLAB is

$$\boxed{\texttt{v = } InitialValue : Increment : FinalValue}$$

The three values in the above assignment can also be valid MATLAB expressions. If no increment is specified, MATLAB uses the default increment of 1.

Examples:

`a = 0:10:100`	produces $a = [\ 0 \quad 10 \quad 20 \quad \ldots \quad 100\ ]$,
`b = 0:pi/50:2*pi`	produces $b = [\ 0 \quad \frac{\pi}{50} \quad \frac{2\pi}{50} \quad \ldots \quad 2\pi\ ]$,
	i.e., a linearly-spaced vector from 0 to 2π spaced at $\pi/50$,
`u = 2:10`	produces $a = [\ 2 \quad 3 \quad 4 \quad \ldots \quad 10\ ]$.

As you may notice, no square brackets are required if a vector is generated this way, however, a vector assignment such as `u = [1:10 33:-2:19]` does require square brackets to force the concatenation of the two vectors: `[1 2 3 ... 10]` and `[33 31 29 ... 19]`. Finally, we mention the use of two frequently used built-in functions to generate vectors:

`linspace(a,b,n)`	generates a linearly spaced vector of length n from a to b.
	Example: `u=linspace(0,20,5)` generates `u=[0 5 10 15 20]`.
	Thus `u=linspace(a,b,n)` is the same as `u=a:(b-a)/(n-1):b`.
`logspace(a,b,n)`	generates a logarithmically spaced vector of length n
	from 10^a to 10^b.
	Example: `v=logspace(0,3,4)` generates `v=[1 10 100 1000]`.
	Thus `logspace(a,b,n)` is the same as `10.^(linspace(a,b,n))`.
	(The array operation `.^` is discussed in the next section.)

Special vectors, such as vectors of zeros or ones of a specific length, can be created with the utility matrix functions **zeros**, **ones**, etc.

Examples:

`u = zeros(1,1000)`	initializes a 1000 element long row vector
`v = ones(10,1)`	creates a 10 element long column vector of 1's.

3.2 Matrix and Array Operations

On-line help category: ops

3.2.1 Arithmetic operations

For people who are used to programming in a conventional language like Pascal, Fortran, or C, it is an absolute delight to be able to write a matrix product as C = A*B where A is an $m \times n$ matrix and B is an $n \times k$ matrix [2]. MATLAB allows all arithmetic operations:

On-line help topic: arith

+	addition
−	subtraction
*	multiplication
/	division
^ (caret)	exponentiation

to be carried out on matrices in straightforward ways as long as the operation makes sense mathematically and the operands are compatible. Thus,

A+B or A−B	is valid if A and B are of the same size,
A*B	is valid if A's number of columns equals B's number of rows,
A/B	is tricky but valid, and equals $A \cdot B^{-1}$ for same-size square matrices A and B,
A^2	makes sense only if A is square, and equals A*A.

In all the above commands if B is replaced by a scalar, say α, the arithmetic operations are still carried out. In this case, the command A+α adds α to each element of A, the command A*α (or α*A) multiplies each element of A by α and so on. Vectors, of course, are just treated as a single row or a column matrix and therefore a command such as w = u*v, where u and v are same size vectors, say $m \times 1$, produces an error (because you cannot multiply an $m \times 1$ matrix with an $m \times 1$ matrix) while w = u*v$'$ and w = u$'$*v execute correctly, producing the inner and outer product of the two vectors respectively (see examples in Fig 3.3).

The right division: In addition to the normal or *left* division (/), there is a *right* division (\) in MATLAB. This division is used to solve a matrix equation. In particular, the command x = A\b solves the matrix equation **A x = b**. Thus A\b is *almost* the same as inv(A)*b, but faster and more numerically stable than computing inv(A)*b. In the degenerate case of scalars 5\3 gives 0.6, which is 3/5 or $5^{-1} * 3$.

---

[2]although you can do C = A*B in C^{++}.

On-line
help
category:
`arith,`
`slash`

Array operation:

How does one get products like $[u_1v_1 \ \ u_2v_2 \ u_3v_3 \ \dots \ u_nv_n]$ from two vectors u and v? No, you do not have to use *DO* or *FOR* loops. You can do *array operation—* operations done on element-by-element basis. Element-by-element multiplication, division, and exponentiation between two matrices or vectors of the same size are done by preceding the corresponding arithmetic operators by a period (.):

.*	element-by-element multiplication
./	element-by-element left division
.\	element-by-element right division
.^	element-by-element exponentiation
.'	nonconjugated transpose

Examples:

`u.*v`	produces	$[u_1v_1 \ \ u_2v_2 \ u_3v_3 \ \dots],$
`u./v`	produces	$[u_1/v_1 \ \ u_2/v_2 \ u_3/v_3 \ \dots],$ and
`u.^v`	produces	$[u_1^{v_1}, \ u_2^{v_2}, \ u_3^{v_3}, \ \dots].$

The same is true for matrices. For two same-sized matrices A and B, the command `C = A.*B` produces a matrix C with elements $C_{ij} = A_{ij}B_{ij}$. Clearly, there is a big difference between `A^2` and `A.^2` (see Fig. 3.3). Once again, scalars do enjoy a special status. While `u./v` or `u.^v` will produce an error if u and v are not the same size, `1./v` happily computes $[1/v_1 \ 1/v_2 \ 1/v_3 \ \dots]$, and `pi.^v` gives $[\pi^{v_1} \ \pi^{v_2} \ \pi^{v_3} \ \dots].$

On-line
help
topic:
`relop`

3.2.2   Relational operations

There are six relational operators in MATLAB:

<	less than
<=	less than or equal
>	greater than
>=	greater than or equal
==	equal
~=	not equal.

These operations result in a vector or matrix of the same size as the operands, with 1 where the relation is true and 0 where it is false.

Examples: If $x = [1 \ \ 5 \ 3 \ 7]$ and $y = [0 \ \ 2 \ 8 \ 7]$, then

```
>>A=[1 2 3; 4 5 6; 7 8 9];
>>x=A(1,:)'

x =

    1
    2
    3
```

Matrices are transposed using the single right quote character ('). Here x is the transpose of the first row of A.

```
>>x'*x

ans =

   14
```

Matrix or vector products are well-defined between compatible pairs. A row vector (x') times a column vector (x) of the same length gives the inner product, which is a scalar...

```
>>x*x'

ans =

    1    2    3
    2    4    6
    3    6    9
```

... but a column vector times a row vector of the same length gives the outer product, which is a matrix.

```
>>A*x

ans =

   14
   32
   50
```

Look how easy it is to multiply a vector with a matrix-- compare to Fortran or Pascal.

```
>>A^2

ans =

    30    36    42
    66    81    96
   102   126   150
```

You can even exponentiate a matrix if it is a square matrix. A^2 is simply A*A.

```
>>A.^2

ans =

     1     4     9
    16    25    36
    49    64    81
```

When a dot precedes the arithmatic operators *, ^, and /, MATLAB performs array operations (element-by-element operations). So, A.^2 produces a matrix with elements $(a_{ij})^2$.

Figure 3.3: Examples of matrix transpose, matrix multiplication, matrix exponentiation, and array exponentiation.

`k = x < y`	results in $k = [0\ 0\ 1\ 0]$	because $x_i < y_i$ for $i = 3$,
`k = x <= y`	results in $k = [0\ 0\ 1\ 1]$	because $x_i \leq y_i$ for $i = 3$ and 4,
`k = x > y`	results in $k = [1\ 1\ 0\ 0]$	because $x_i > y_i$ for $i = 1$ and 2,
`k = x >= y`	results in $k = [1\ 1\ 0\ 1]$	because $x_i \geq y_i$ for $i = 1, 2$ and 4,
`k = x == y`	results in $k = [0\ 0\ 0\ 1]$	because $x_i = y_i$ for $i = 4$, and
`k = x ~= y`	results in $k = [1\ 1\ 1\ 0]$	because $x_i \neq y_i$ for $i = 1, 2$ and 3.

Although these operations are usually used in conditional statements such as *if-then-else* to branch out to different cases, they can be used to do pretty sophisticated matrix manipulation. For example, `u = v(v >= sin(pi/3))` finds all elements of vector v such that $v_i \geq \sin\frac{\pi}{3}$ and stores them in vector u. Two or more of these operations can also be combined with the help of *logical operators* (described below).

On-line help topic: `relop`

3.2.3   Logical operations

There are four logical operators:

`&`	logical AND
`|`	logical OR
`~`	logical complement (NOT)
`xor`	exclusive OR

These operators work pretty much like the relational operators and produce vectors or matrices of the same size as the operands, with 1 where the condition is true and 0 where false.

Examples: For two vectors $x = [0\ 5\ 3\ 7]$ and $y = [0\ 2\ 8\ 7]$,

`m = (x>y)&(x>4)`	results in $m = [0\ 1\ 0\ 0]$	because the condition is true only for x_2.
`n = x|y`	results in $n = [0\ 1\ 1\ 1]$	because either x_i or y_i is non-zero. for $i = 2, 3$ and 4.
`m = ~(x|y)`	results in $m = [1\ 0\ 0\ 0]$	which is the logical complement of `x|y`.
`p = xor(x,y)`	results in $p = [0\ 0\ 0\ 0]$	because there is no such index i for which x_i or y_i, but not both, is non-zero.

Since the output of the logical operations is a 0-1 vector or a 0-1 matrix, the output can be used as the index of a matrix to extract appropriate elements. For example, to see those elements of x that satisfy both the conditions `(x > y) & (x > 4)`, type `x((x>y) &(x>4))`.

There are also many useful built-in logical functions:

`all`	true $(= 1)$ if all elements of a vector are true.
	Example: `all(x<0)` returns 1 if each element of x is negative.
`any`	true $(= 1)$ if any element of a vector is true.
	Example: `any(x)` returns 1 if any element of x is non-zero.
`exist`	true $(= 1)$ if the argument (a variable or a function) exists.
`isempty`	true $(= 1)$ for an empty matrix.
`isinf`	true for all infinite elements of a matrix.
`isfinite`	true for all finite elements of a matrix.
`isnan`	true for all elements of a matrix that are Not-A-Number.
`find`	finds indices of non-zero elements of a matrix.
	Examples: `find(x)` returns [2 3 4] for `x=[0 2 5 7]`,
	`i=find(x>5)` returns $i = 4$.
	`[r,c] = find(A>100)` returns the row and column indices i and j of A, in vectors `r` and `c`, for which $A_{ij} > 100$.

To complete this list of logical functions, we just mention `isreal`, `issparse`, `isstr`, and `isglobal`.

3.2.4 Elementary math functions

On-line help category: `elfun`

All of the following built-in math functions take matrix inputs and perform array operations (element-by-element) on them. Thus, they produce an output matrix of the same size as the input matrix.

Trigonometric functions

`sin`	Sine.	`sinh`	Hyperbolic sine.
`asin`	Inverse sine.	`asinh`	Inverse hyperbolic sine.
`cos`	Cosine.	`cosh`	Hyperbolic cosine.
`acos`	Inverse cosine.	`acosh`	Inverse hyperbolic cosine.
`tan`	Tangent.	`tanh`	Hyperbolic tangent.
`atan,atan2`	Inverse tangent.	`atanh`	Inverse hyperbolic tangent.
`sec`	Secant.	`sech`	Hyperbolic secant.
`asec`	Inverse secant.	`asech`	Inverse hyperbolic secant.
`csc`	Cosecant.	`csch`	Hyperbolic cosecant.
`acsc`	Inverse cosecant.	`acsch`	Inverse hyperbolic cosecant.
`cot`	Cotangent.	`coth`	Hyperbolic cotangent.
`acot`	Inverse cotangent.	`acoth`	Inverse hyperbolic cotangent.

The angles given to these functions as arguments must be in radians. All of these functions, except `atan2`, take a single scalar, vector, or matrix as input argument. The function `atan2` takes two input arguments: `atan2(y,x)` and produces the four quadrant inverse tangent such that $-\pi \leq \tan^{-1}\frac{y}{x} \leq \pi$. This gives the angle in a rectangular to polar conversion.

Examples: If `q=[0 pi/2 pi]`, `x=[1 -1 -1 1]`, and `y=[1 1 -1 -1]`, then

> `sin(q)`   gives `[0 1 0]`,
>
> `sinh(q)`   gives `[0 2.3013 11.5487]`,
>
> `atan(y./x)` gives `[0.7854 -0.7854 0.7854 -0.7854]`, and
>
> `atan2(y,x)` gives `[0.7854 2.3562 -2.3562 -0.7854]`.

Exponential functions

`exp`	Exponential.
	Example: `exp(A)` produces a matrix with elements $e^{(A_{ij})}$.
	So how do you compute e^A? See the next section.
`log`	Natural logarithm.
	Example: `log(A)` produces a matrix with elements $\ln(A_{ij})$.
`log10`	Base 10 logarithm.
	Example: `log10(A)` produces a matrix with elements $\log_{10}(A_{ij})$.
`sqrt`	Square root.
	Example: `sqrt(A)` produces a matrix with elements $\sqrt{A_{ij}}$.
	But what about $\sqrt{A}$? See the next section.

Clearly, these are array operations. You can, however, also compute matrix exponential e^A, matrix square root $\sqrt{A}$, etc. See the next section (Section 3.2.5).

Complex functions

`abs`	Absolute value.
	Example: `exp(A)` produces a matrix of absolute values $|A_{ij}|$.
`angle`	Phase angle.
	Example: `angle(A)` gives the phase angles of the complex matrix A.
`conj`	Complex conjugate.
	Example: `conj(A)` produces a matrix with elements $\bar{A}_{ij}$.
`imag`	Imaginary part.
	Example: `imag(A)` extracts the imaginary part of A.

real   Real part.

                Example: real(A) extracts the real part of A.

Round-off functions

fix   Round towards 0.

                Example: fix([-2.33 2.66]) $= [-2 \quad 2]$.

floor   Round towards $-\infty$.

                Example: floor([-2.33 2.66]) $= [-3 \quad 2]$.

ceil   Round towards $+\infty$.

                Example: ceil([-2.33 2.66]) $= [-2 \quad 3]$.

round   Round towards the nearest integer.

                Example: round([-2.33 2.66]) $= [-2 \quad 3]$.

rem   Remainder after division. rem(a,b) is the same as a - fix(a./b).

                Example: If a=[-1.5 7], b=[2 3], then rem(a,b) = [-1.5 1].

sign   Signum function.

                Example: sign([-2.33 2.66]) $= [-1 \quad 1]$.

3.2.5   Matrix functions

On-line help category: matfun

We discussed the difference between the array exponentiation A.^2 and the matrix exponentiation A^2 above. There are some built-in functions that are truly matrix functions, and that also have array counterparts. The matrix functions are:

expm(A)   finds the exponential of matrix A, e^A,

logm(A)   finds $\log(A)$ such that $A = e^{\log(A)}$,

sqrtm(A)   finds $\sqrt{A}$.

The array counterparts of these functions are exp, log, and sqrt, which operate on each element of the input matrix (see Fig. 3.4 for examples). The matrix exponential function expm also has some specialized variants expm1, expm2, and expm3. See on-line help or the Reference Guide [2] for their proper usage. MATLAB also provides a general matrix function funm for evaluating true matrix functions.

```
>>A=[1 2; 3 4];

A =

       1       2
       3       4

>>asqrt = sqrt(A)

asqrt =

     1.0000    1.4142
     1.7321    2.0000

>>Asqrt = sqrtm(A)

Asqrt =

    0.5537 + 0.4644i    0.8070 - 0.2124i
    1.2104 - 0.3186i    1.7641 + 0.1458i

>>exp_aij = exp(A)

exp_aij =

     2.7183    7.3891
    20.0855   54.5982

>>exp_A = expm(A)

exp_A =

    51.9690    74.7366
   112.1048   164.0738
```

sqrt is an array operation. It gives the square root of each element of A as is evident from the output here.

sqrtm, on the other hand, is a true matrix function, i.e., it computes $\sqrt{A}$. Thus [Asqrt]*[Asqrt] = [A].

Similarly, exp gives element-by-element exponential of the matrix, whereas expm finds the true matrix exponential e^A. For info on other matrix functions, type
help matfun.

Figure 3.4: Examples of differences between matrix functions and array functions.

3.2.6   Character strings

On-line help category: strfun.

All character strings are entered within two single right quote characters—'*string*'. MATLAB treats every string as a row vector with one element per character. For example, typing

message = 'Leave me alone'

creates a vector, named **message**, of size 1×14 (spaces in strings count as characters). Therefore, to create a column vector of text objects, each text string must have exactly the same number of characters. For example, the command

names = ['John'; 'Ravi'; 'Mary'; 'Xiao']

creates a column vector with one name per row, although, to MATLAB, the variable **names** is a 4×4 matrix. Clearly, the command howdy = ['Hi'; 'Hello'; 'Namaste'] will result in an error because each row has different length. Text strings of different lengths can be made to be of equal length by padding them with blanks. Thus the correct input for **howdy** will be

howdy = ['Hi '; 'Hello '; 'Namaste']

with each string being 7 characters long ($_\sqcup$ denotes a space).

An easier way of doing the same thing is to use the command **str2mat**, which converts strings to a matrix. **str2mat(s1,s2,...)** puts each string argument **s1, s2,** etc., up to 10 arguments, in a row and creates a string matrix by padding each row with appropriate number of blanks. Thus, to create the same **howdy** as above, we type

howdy = str2mat('Hi','Hello','Namaste')

Since the same quote character (the single right quote) is used to signal the beginning as well as the end of a string, this character cannot be used inside a string for a quote or apostrophe. For a quote within a string you must use the double quote character ("). Thus, to title a graph with *3-D View of Boomerang's Path* you write

title('3-D View of Boomerang"s Path').

Manipulating character strings

Character strings can be manipulated just like matrices. Thus,

c = [howdy(2,:) names(3,:)]

produces **Hello Mary** as the output in variable c. This feature can be used along with number-to-string conversion functions, such as **num2str** and **int2str**, to create text objects containing dynamic values of variables. Such text objects are particularly useful in creating titles for figures and other graphics annotation commands (see Section 5). For example, suppose you want to produce a few variance-study graphs with different values of the sample size n, an integer variable. Producing the title of the graph with the command

```
title(['Variance study with sample size n = ',int2str(n)])
```

writes titles with the current value of n printed in the title.

There are several built-in functions for character string manipulation:

abs	converts characters to their ASCII numeric values,
blanks(n)	creates n blank characters,
deblank	removes the trailing blanks from a string,
eval	executes the string as a command (see description below),
findstr	finds the specified substring in a given string,
int2str	converts integers to strings (see example above),
isstring	true $(= 1)$ if the argument is a string,
lower	converts any upper case letters in the string to lower case
num2str	converts numbers to strings (similar to int2str),
str2mat	converts strings to a matrix using automatic padding,
strcmp	compares two strings, returns 1 if same,
upper	converts any lower case letters in the string to upper case.

The eval function

MATLAB provides a powerful function eval to *evaluate* text strings and execute them if they contain valid MATLAB commands. For example, the command

```
eval('x = 5*sin(pi/3)')
```

computes $x = 5\sin(\pi/3)$ and is equivalent to typing x = 5*sin(pi/3) on the command prompt.

There are many uses of the eval function. One use of this function is in creating or loading sequentially numbered data files. For example, you can use eval to run a set of commands ten times while you take a two-hour lunch break. The following script runs the set of commands ten times and saves the output variables in ten different files.

```
% Example of use of EVAL function
% A script file that lets you go out for lunch while MATLAB slogs
%----------------------
for k = 1:10
    outputfile = ['result',int2str(k)];  % see explanation below
    :
    % write commands to run your function here
    :
    x = ....                            % compute x
    y = ....                            % compute y
    z = ....                            % compute z
    % now save variables x, y, and z in a Mat-file
    eval(['save ',outputfile,' x y z'])  % see explanation below
end
```

The commands used above are a little subtle. So read them carefully. In particular, note that

- The first command, `outputfile = ...`, creates a name by combining the counter of the `for`-loop with the string `result`, thus producing the names `result1, result2, result3`, etc. as the loop counter k takes the values 1, 2, 3, etc.

- The last command `eval(...)` has *one* input argument—a long string that is made up of three strings: `'save '`, `outputfile`, and `' x y z'`. Note that while `save` and `x, y, z` are enclosed within quotes to make them character strings, the variable `outputfile` is not enclosed within quotes because it is already a string.

- The square brackets inside the `eval` command are used here to produce a single string by concatenating three individual strings. The brackets are not a part of the `eval` command. Note the blank spaces in the strings `'save '` and `' x y z'`. These spaces are essential. Can you see why? [Hint: Try to produce the string with and without the spaces.]

Similar to `eval` there is a function `feval` for evaluating functions. See page 81 for a discussion on `feval`.

On-line
help
category:
help

3.3   Using Built-in Functions and help

MATLAB provides hundreds of built-in functions for numerical linear algebra, data analysis, Fourier transforms, data interpolation and curve fitting, root-finding, numerical solution of ordinary differential equations, numerical quadrature, sparse matrix calculations, and general-purpose graphics. There is on-line help for all built-in functions. Although the help facility in MATLAB 4.x is improved over the previous versions, it could still use some help of its own to serve the users better. The menu-driven help for PCs and Macs is better than the one for Unix machines and is a step in the right direction. With so many built-in functions and not-so-great on-line help, it is important to know how to look for functions and how to learn to use them. There are two ways to get help:

- **If you know the exact name of a function**, you can get help on it by typing help *functionname* on the command line. For example, typing help help provides help on the function help itself.

- **If you are looking for a function**, use lookfor *keyword* to get a list of functions with the string *keyword* in their description. For example, typing lookfor 'identity matrix' lists functions (there are two of them) that create identity matrices.

Typing help by itself brings out a list of categories (see Fig. 3.5) in which help is organized. You can get help on one of these categories by typing help *category*. For example, typing help elfun gives a list of elementary math functions with a very brief description of each function. Further help can now be obtained on a function because the exact name of the function is now known.

On the other hand, lookfor is a friendlier command. It lets you specify a descriptive word about the function for which you need help. The following example takes you through the process of looking for help on finding eigenvalues of a matrix, getting help on the exact function that serves the purpose, and using the function in the correct way to get the results.

Caution: MATLAB's help command is not forgiving of any typos or misspellings, and hence you must know the exact command name.

```
>>help
                              help by itself lists the names of categories in
HELP topics:                  which the on-line help files are organized.

matlab:general        -   General purpose commands.
matlab:ops            -   Operators and special characters.
matlab:lang           -   Language constructs and debugging.
matlab:elmat          -   Elementary matrices and matrix manipulation.
matlab:specmat        -   Specialized matrices.
matlab:elfun          -   Elementary math functions.
matlab:specfun        -   Specialized math functions.
matlab:matfun         -   Matrix functions - numerical linear algebra.
matlab:datafun        -   Data analysis and Fourier transform functions.
matlab:polyfun        -   Polynomial and interpolation functions.
matlab:funfun         -   Function functions - nonlinear numerical methods
matlab:sparfun        -   Sparse matrix functions.
matlab:plotxy         -   Two dimensional graphics.
matlab:plotxyz        -   Three dimensional graphics.
matlab:graphics       -   General purpose graphics functions.
matlab:color          -   Color control and lighting model functions.
matlab:sounds         -   Sound processing functions.
matlab:strfun         -   Character string functions.
matlab:iofun          -   Low-level file I/O functions.
matlab:demos          -   The MATLAB Expo and other demonstrations.
Toolbox:local         -   Local function library.
MATLAB 4.1:Extern     -   (No table of contents file)
Macintosh HD:MATLAB 4.1 - (No table of contents file)

For more help on directory/topic, type "help topic".

                              help category  lists the functions in that cate-
>> help funfun                gory. Detailed help can then be obtained by
                              typing: help functionname.

Function functions - nonlinear numerical methods.
Copyright (c) 1984-93 by The MathWorks, Inc.

   ode23       - Solve differential equations, low order method.
   ode23p      - Solve and plot solutions.
   ode45       - Solve differential equations, high order method.
   quad        - Numerically evaluate integral, low order method.
   quad8       - Numerically evaluate integral, high order method.
   fmin        - Minimize function of one variable.
   fmins       - Minimize function of several variables.
   fzero       - Find zero of function of one variable.
   fplot       - Plot function.

See also The Optimization Toolbox, which has a comprehensive
set of function functions for optimizing and minimizing functions.
```

Figure 3.5: MATLAB help facility.

3.3.1   Example–1: Finding eigenvalues and eigenvectors

Suppose we are interested in finding out the eigenvalues and eigenvectors of a matrix A, but we do not know what functions MATLAB provides for this purpose. Since we do not know the exact name of the required function, our best bet to get help is to try `lookfor eigenvalue`. Figure 3.6 shows MATLAB's response to this command.

```
>> lookfor eigenvalue        lookfor provides keyword search for
                             help files containing the search string.

ROSSER A classic symmetric eigenvalue test problem.
WILKINSON Wilkinson's eigenvalue test matrix.
BALANCE Diagonal scaling to improve eigenvalue accuracy.
EIG  Eigenvalues and eigenvectors.
EXPM3 Matrix exponential via eigenvalues and eigenvectors.
POLYEIG Polynomial eigenvalue problem.
QZ   Generalized eigenvalues.
EIGMOVIE Symmetric eigenvalue movie.
EIGENSYS Symbolic matrix eigenvalues and eigenvectors.

>> help eig                  Detailed help can then be obtained on
                             any of the listed files with  help.

 EIG  Eigenvalues and eigenvectors.
   EIG(X) is a vector containing the eigenvalues of a square
   matrix X.

   [V,D] = EIG(X) produces a diagonal matrix D of
   eigenvalues and a full matrix V whose columns are the
   corresponding eigenvectors so that X*V = V*D.

   [V,D] = EIG(X,'nobalance') performs the computation with
   balancing disabled, which sometimes gives more accurate
   results for certain problems with unusual scaling.

   Generalized eigenvalues and eigenvectors.

   EIG(A,B) is a vector containing the generalized
   eigenvalues of square matrices A and B.

   [V,D] = EIG(A,B) produces a diagonal matrix D of general-
   ized eigenvalues and a full matrix V whose columns are
   the corresponding eigenvectors so that A*V = B*V*D.
```

Figure 3.6: Example of use of on-line help.

As shown in Fig. 3.6, MATLAB lists all functions that have the string 'eigenvalue' either in their name or in the first line of their description. You can then browse through the list, pick the function that seems closest to your needs, and ask for further help on it. In Fig. 3.6, for example, we seek help on function `eig`. The on-line help on `eig` tells us what this function does and how to use it.

Thus, if we are interested in just the eigenvalues of a matrix A, we type `eig(A)` to get the eigenvalues, but if we want to find both the eigenvalues and the eigenvectors of A, we specify the output list explicitly and type `[eigvec, eigval] = eig(A)` (see Fig. 3.7). The names of the output or the input variables can, of course, be anything we choose. Although it's obvious, we note that the list of the variables (input or output) must be in the same order as specified by the function.

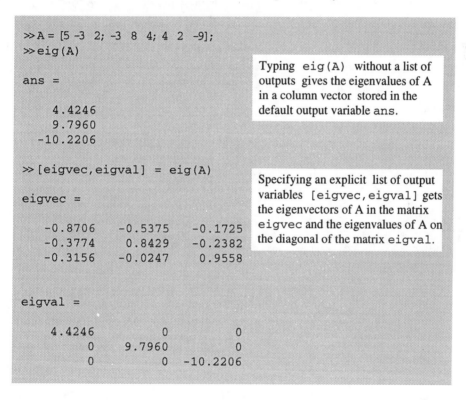

```
>> A = [5 -3  2; -3  8  4; 4  2  -9];
>> eig(A)

ans =

      4.4246
      9.7960
    -10.2206

>> [eigvec,eigval] = eig(A)

eigvec =

    -0.8706    -0.5375    -0.1725
    -0.3774     0.8429    -0.2382
    -0.3156    -0.0247     0.9558

eigval =

      4.4246          0          0
           0     9.7960          0
           0          0   -10.2206
```

Typing `eig(A)` without a list of outputs gives the eigenvalues of A in a column vector stored in the default output variable ans.

Specifying an explicit list of output variables `[eigvec,eigval]` gets the eigenvectors of A in the matrix `eigvec` and the eigenvalues of A on the diagonal of the matrix `eigval`.

Figure 3.7: Examples of use of the function `eig` to find eigenvalues and eigenvectors of a matrix.

3.3.2   Example–2: Solving a system of linear equations

One of the greatest strengths of MATLAB is its linear algebra package. For matrix analysis, eigenvalue analysis, and solution of linear systems, the functions provided and their ease of use are simply incredible.

There are many ways to solve a system of linear algebraic equations in MATLAB. Unfortunately, typing `lookfor 'linear equations'` lists only one function, `linsolve`. But by typing `help matfun` (`matfun` is the help category for matrix functions), you get a list of many functions used in linear algebra, along with brief descriptive notes. In this list there is a sublist of functions under the heading *Linear equations*. These functions are designed for solving various linear systems. While matrix factorization functions such as `lu, chol, qr` can be used in appropriate cases to solve a system of equations, solving a simple system such as $\mathbf{A}\,\mathbf{x} = \mathbf{b}$ is as simple as typing `x = A\b`. As an example, Fig. 3.8 shows the solution of the following system of equations.

$$\begin{bmatrix} 5 & -3 & 2 \\ -3 & 8 & 4 \\ 2 & 4 & -9 \end{bmatrix} \begin{Bmatrix} x_1 \\ x_2 \\ x_3 \end{Bmatrix} = \begin{Bmatrix} 10 \\ 20 \\ 9 \end{Bmatrix} \tag{3.1}$$

```
>>A = [5 -3 2; -3 8 4; 2 4 -9];    % Enter matrix A
>>b = [10; 20; 9];                 % Enter column vector B
>>x = A\b                          % Solve for x.

x =
```
The backslash (\) or the left division is used to solve a linear system of equations [A]{x} = {b}. For more information type: `help slash`.
```
    3.4442
    3.1982
    1.1868
```

Figure 3.8: Example of solution of a linear system of equations $\mathbf{A}\,\mathbf{x} = \mathbf{b}$.

The command `x = A\b` computes the solution of the system by Gaussian elimination. For more information on '\', type `help slash`. You could also solve the system with the command `x = inv(A)*b`, although using explicit inverse of a matrix for solving a linear system is wasteful of cpu cycles and generally less accurate. To check your answer you can compute `A*x` and compare with b. In a typical linear algebra course, one of the methods you learn to solve a linear system is by row-reducing the associated matrix. You can row-reduce a matrix in MATLAB with the function `rref` (the acronym stands for row reduced echelon form). Thus you could also find the solution of Eqn. 3.1 by typing

```
A = [5 -3 2; -3 8 4; 2 4 -9];
b = [10; 20; 9];
B = [A b];
C = rref(B)
```

(or equivalently, `C = rref([A b])`). The solution is the last column of the row reduced matrix C.

Some comments on the help facility:

- MATLAB is case-sensitive. All built-in functions in MATLAB use lowercase letters for their names, yet the `help` on any function lists the function in uppercase letters, as is evident from Figs. 3.5 and 3.6. For the first-time user, it may be frustrating to type the command exactly as shown by the help facility, i.e., in uppercase, only to receive an error message from MATLAB.

- On-line help can be obtained by typing help commands on the command line, as we have described in the foregoing section. This method is applicable on all platforms that support MATLAB. In addition, on some computers such as Macintosh and IBM compatibles with Windows, on-line help is also available on the menu bar. For example, on Macs, MATLAB HELP is available under Balloon Help in the top right corner of the menu bar. One can scroll through the help files by selecting and clicking with the mouse.

- Although `lookfor` is a good command to find help if you are uncertain about the name of the function you want, it has an annoying drawback: it takes only one string as an argument. So typing `lookfor linear equations` causes an error (but `lookfor 'linear equations'` is ok), while both `lookfor linear` and `lookfor equations` do return useful help.

On-line
help
category:
general

3.4   Saving and Loading Data

There are many ways of saving and loading data in MATLAB. The most direct way is to use the `save` and `load` commands. You can also save a session or part of a session, including data and commands, using the `diary` command. We will describe `save` and `load` first.

3.4.1   Saving into and loading from the binary Mat-files

The `save` command can be used to save either the entire workspace or a few selected variables in a file called *Mat-file*. Mat-files are written in binary format with full 16 bit precision. It is also possible to write data in Mat-files in 8-digit or 16-digit ASCII format with optional arguments to the `save` command (see on-line help). Mat-files must always have a '.mat' extension. The data saved in these files can be loaded into the MATLAB workspace by the `load` command. Examples of proper usage of these commands are as follows:

`save tubedata.mat x y`	saves variables `x` and `y` in the file `tubedata.mat`.
`save newdata rx ry rz`	saves variables `rx`, `ry`, and `rz` in the file `newdata.mat`. Here MATLAB automatically supplies the '.mat' extension to the file name.
`save xdata.dat x -ascii`	saves variable `x` in the file `xdata.dat` in 8-digit ASCII format.
`save`	saves the entire workspace in the file `matlab.mat`.
`load tubedata`	loads the variables saved in the file `tubedata.mat`.
`load`	loads the variables saved in the default file `matlab.mat`.

ASCII data files can also be loaded into the MATLAB workspace with the `load` command provided the data file contains only a rectangular matrix of numbers. For more information, see on-line help on `load`.

You can also use cut-and-paste between the MATLAB command window and other applications (such as Microsoft Excel) to import and export data. Figure 3.9 shows an example session with `save` and `load` commands.

```
>>whos                                    Check what variables are in the workspace.
        Name        Size      Elements      Bytes    Density   Complex

           A        5 by 5          25        200      Full        No
       state        5 by 20        100        800      Full        No
      strain        20 by 1         20        160      Full        No
      stress        20 by 1         20        160      Full        No

Grand total is 165 elements using 1320 bytes

leaving 7070224 bytes of memory free.
                                          Save variables state, stress,
>>save myheadache state stress strain     and strain in the Mat-file named
                                          myheadache.mat.

>>clear                                   Clear the entire workspace.

>>whos                                    Check if the workspace is cleared.



leaving 7045968 bytes of memory free.

>>load myheadache                         Load the file myheadache.mat.

>>whos                                    Check if all variables saved in the
                                          file are loaded in the workspace.
        Name        Size      Elements      Bytes    Density   Complex

       state        5 by 20        100        800      Full        No
      strain        20 by 1         20        160      Full        No
      stress        20 by 1         20        160      Full        No

Grand total is 140 elements using 1120 bytes.....
```

Figure 3.9: Example of a session on saving and loading data using Mat-files.

3.4.2   Recording a session with diary

An entire MATLAB session, or a part of one, can be recorded in a user-editable file, by means of the `diary` command. A file name with any extension can be specified as the output file. For example, typing `diary session1.out` opens a diary file named `session1.out`. Everything in the command window, including user-input, MATLAB output, error messages etc., that follows the diary command is recorded in the file `session1.out`. The recording is terminated by the command `diary off`. The same diary file can be opened later during the same session by typing `diary on`. This will append the subsequent part of the session to the same file `session1.out`. All the figures in this book that show commands typed in the command window and consequent MATLAB output were generated with the diary command. Diary files may be opened and modified with any standard text editor.

The contents of a diary file can be loaded into the MATLAB workspace by converting the diary file into a *script file* (see Section 4.1 for more details on script files) and then executing the script file in MATLAB. To do this, we must first edit the diary file to remove all unwanted lines (for example, MATLAB error messages) and output generated by commands, and then we must rename the file with a '.m' extension, to make it a script file. Now, we can execute the file by typing the name of the file (without the '.m' extension) at the command prompt. This will execute all the commands in the diary file. Thus, it is also possible to load the values of a variable that were written explicitly in a diary file. If the variables were from an array, we would need to enclose them in square brackets, and assign this to a variable. Values loaded this way will have only the precision explicitly written in the diary file. The number of digits of a variable recorded in the diary depends on the `format` in effect at the time (for a description of `format`, see Section 1.6.3). Therefore, we do not recommend this method of saving and loading MATLAB-generated-data. The diary is a good way of recording a session to be included in reports or to show someone how a particular set of calculations was done.

As an alternative to the *diary* facility, you can scroll through the command window and copy (the *cut-and-paste* method) the parts you want to a text file. Better yet, if you are a PC or a Mac user and you have Microsoft Word 6.0 or later, you can create a fancy **Notebook** —a Word document with embedded MATLAB commands and output, including graphics. To do this you must also have a version of MATLAB that supports the *Notebook* facility.

3.5 Plotting simple graphs

We close this section on interactive computation with an example of how to plot a simple graph and save it as an Encapsulated PostScript file.

As mentioned in the introduction, the plots in MATLAB appear in the graphics window. MATLAB provides very good facilities for both 2-D and 3-D graphics. The commands to produce simple plots are surprisingly simple. For complicated graphics and special effects there are a lot of built-in functions that enable the user to manipulate the graphics window in many ways. Unfortunately, the more control you want the more complicated it gets. We describe the graphics facility in more detail in Chapter 5.

The most direct command to produce a graph in 2-D is the `plot` command. If a variable `ydata` has n values corresponding to n values of variable `xdata`, then `plot(xdata,ydata)` produces a plot with `xdata` on the horizontal axis and `ydata` on the vertical axis. To produce overlay plots, you can specify any number of pairs of vectors as the argument of the `plot` command. But we discuss more of this, and much more on other aspects of plotting, in Section 5. Figure 3.10 shows an example of plotting a simple graph of $f(t) = e^{t/10} \sin(t)$, $0 \le t \le 20$. This function could also be plotted using `fplot`, a command for plotting functions of a single variable. The most important thing to remember about the `plot` command is that the vector inputs for the x-axis data and the y-axis data must be of the same length. Thus, in the command `plot(x1,y1,x2,y2)`, $x1$, and $y1$ must have the same length, $x2$, and $y2$ must have the same length, while $x1$, and $x2$ may have different lengths.

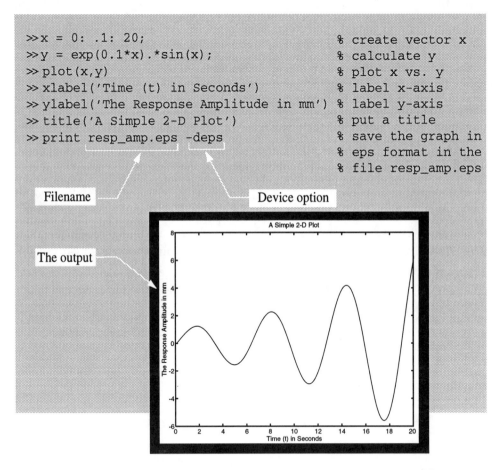

Figure 3.10: Example of a simple 2-D plot of function $f(t) = e^{t/10}\sin(t)$.

4. *Programming in MATLAB: Scripts and Functions*

On-line
help
category:
`lang`

A distinguishing features of MATLAB is its *ease* of extendability, through user-written programs. MATLAB provides its own language, which incorporates many features from C. In some regards, it is a higher-level language than most common programming languages, such as Pascal, Fortran, and C, meaning that you will spend less time worrying about formalisms and syntax. For the most part, MATLAB's language feels somewhat natural.

In MATLAB you write your programs in *M-files*. M-files are ordinary ASCII text files written in MATLAB's language. They are called M-files because they must have a '.m' at the end of their name (like `myfunction.m`). M-files can be created using any editor or word processing application.

There are two types of M-files—*script* files and *function* files. Now we discuss their purpose and syntax.

4.1 Script Files

A script file is an 'M-file' with a set of valid MATLAB commands in it. A script file is executed by typing the name of the file (without the '.m' extension) on the command line. It is equivalent to typing all the commands stored in the script file, one by one, at the MATLAB prompt. Naturally, script files work on global variables, that is, variables currently present in the workspace. Results obtained from executing script files are left in the workspace.

A script file may contain any number of commands, including those that call built-in functions or functions written by you. Script files are useful when you have to repeat a set of commands several times. Here is an example.

Example of a Script File: Let us write a script file to solve the following system of linear equations:

$$
\begin{bmatrix}
5 & 2r & r \\
3 & 6 & 2r-1 \\
2 & r-1 & 3r
\end{bmatrix}
\begin{Bmatrix}
x_1 \\
x_2 \\
x_3
\end{Bmatrix}
=
\begin{Bmatrix}
2 \\
3 \\
5
\end{Bmatrix}
\tag{4.1}
$$

or $\mathbf{Ax} = \mathbf{b}$. Clearly, $\mathbf{A}$ depends on the parameter r. We want to find the solution of the equation for various values of the parameter r. We also want to find, say, the determinant of matrix $\mathbf{A}$ in each case. Let us write a set of MATLAB commands that do the job, and store these commands in a file called 'solvex.m'. How you create this file, write the commands in it, and save the file, depends on the computer you are using. But in any case, you are creating a file called `solvex.m`, which will be saved on some disk drive in some directory (or folder).

```
%----------- This is the script file 'solvex.m' ------------
% It solves equation (4.1) for x and also calculates det(A).

A = [5 2*r r; 3 6 2*r-1; 2 r-1 3*r];   % create matrix A
b = [2;3;5];                           % create vector b
det_A = det(A)                         % find the determinant
x = A\b                                % find x
```

In this example, we have not put a semicolon at the end of the last two commands. Therefore, the results of these commands will be displayed on the screen when we execute the script file. The results will be stored in variables `det_A` and `x`, and these will be left in the workspace.

Let us now execute the script in MATLAB.

```
>> r = 1;                   % specify a value of r
>> solvex                   % execute the script file solvex.m

det_A =

      64
x =
   -0.0312
    0.2344
    1.6875
```

This is the output. The values of the variables det_A and x appear on the screen because there is no semi-colon at the end of the corresponding lines in the script file.

You may notice that the value of r is assigned outside the script file and yet solvex picks up this value and computes A. This is because all the variables in the MATLAB workspace are available for use within the script files, and all the variables in a script file are left in the MATLAB workspace. Even though the output of solvex is only det_A and x, A and b are also there in your workspace, and you can see them after execution of solvex by typing their names at the MATLAB prompt. So, if you want to do a big set of computations but in the end you want only a few outputs, a script file is not the right choice. What you need in this case is a *function file*.

Caution:

- *NEVER name a script file the same as the name of a variable it computes.* When MATLAB looks for a name, it first searches the list of variables in the workspace. If a variable of the same name as the script file exists, MATLAB will never be able to access the script file. Thus, if you execute a script file xdot.m that computes a variable xdot, then after the first execution the variable xdot exists in the MATLAB workspace. Now if you change something in the script file and execute it again, all you get is the old value of xdot! Your changed script file is not executed because it cannot be accessed as long as the variable xdot exists in the workspace.

- The name of a script file must begin with a letter. The rest of the characters may include digits and the underscore character. You may give long names but MATLAB will take only the first 19 characters. You may not use any periods in the name other than the last one in '.m'. Thus, names such as project_23C.m, cee213_hw5_1.m, and MyHeartThrobsProfile.m are fine but project.23C.m and cee213_hw5.1.m are not legal.

- Be careful with variable names while working with script files, because all variables generated by a script file are left in the workspace, unless you clear them. Avoid name clashes with built-in functions. It is a good idea to first check if a function or script file of the proposed name already exists. You can do this with the command `exist('name')`, which returns zero if nothing with name *name* exists.

4.2 Function Files

A function file is also an m-file, like a script file, except that the variables in a function file are all local. Function files are like programs or subroutines in Fortran, procedures in Pascal, and functions in C. Once you get to know MATLAB well, this is where you are likely to spend most of your time –writing and refining your own function files.

A function file begins with a function definition line, which has a well-defined list of inputs and outputs. Without this line, the file becomes a script file. The syntax of the function definition line is as follows:

> `function` *[output variables]* `=` *function_name(input variables);*

where the *function_name* must be the same as the *filename* (without the '.m' extension) in which the function is written. For example, if the name of the function is `projectile` it must be written and saved in a file with the name `projectile.m`. The function definition line may look slightly different depending on whether there is no output, a single output, or multiple output.

Examples:

Function Definition Line	*File Name*
`function [rho,H,F] = motion(x,y,t);`	`motion.m`
`function [theta] = angleTH(x,y);`	`angleTH.m`
`function theta = THETA(x,y,z);`	`THETA.m`
`function [] = circle(r);`	`circle.m`
`function circle(r);`	`circle.m`

Caution: The first word in the function definition line, `function`, *must be typed in lower case.* A common mistake to is type it as `Function`.

Anatomy of a function file

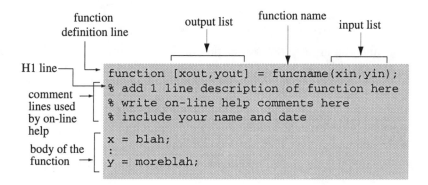

function definition line
output list
function name
input list
H1 line
comment lines used by on-line help
body of the function

```
function [xout,yout] = funcname(xin,yin);
% add 1 line description of function here
% write on-line help comments here
% include your name and date
x = blah;
:
y = moreblah;
```

- Comment lines start with a '%' sign and may be put anywhere. Anything after a % in a line is ignored by MATLAB as a non-executable statement.

- All comment lines immediately following the function definition line are displayed by MATLAB if **help** is sought on the function. The very first comment line immediately following the definition line is called the 'H1' line. An H1 line, if present, is automatically cataloged in the *Contents.m* file of the directory in which the file resides. This allows the line to be referenced by the **lookfor** command. A word of caution: any blanks before the % sign in the first comment line disqualify it from becoming an H1 line. Welcome to the idiosyncrasies of MATLAB!

- A single-output variable is not required to be enclosed in square brackets in the function definition line, but multiple output variables must be enclosed within []. When there is no output variable present, the brackets as well as the equal sign may be omitted (see examples above).

- Input variable names given in the function definition line are local to the function, so other variable names or values can be used in the function call. The name of another function can also be passed as an input variable. No special treatment is required for the function names as input variables in the function definition line. However, when the function is executed, the name of the input function must be passed as a character string, i.e., enclosed within two single right quotes (see example in the next section).

4.2.1   Executing a function

There are two ways a function can be executed, whether it is built-in or user-written:

1. **With explicit output:** This is the full syntax of calling a function. Both the output and the input list are specified in the call. For example, if the function definition line of a function reads

   ```
   function [rho,H,F] = motion(x,y,t);
   ```
   then all the following commands represent legal call (execution) statements:

   - `[r,angmom,force] = motion(xt,yt,time);`   The input variables `xt`, `yt`, and `time` must be defined before executing this command.

   - `[r,h,f] = motion(rx,ry,[0:100]);`   The input variables `rx` and `ry` must be defined beforehand, the third input variable `t` is specified in the call statement.

   - `[r,h,f] = motion(2,3.5,0.001);`   All input values are specified in the call statement.

   - `[radius,h] = motion(rx,ry);`   Call with partial list of input and output. The third input variable must be assigned a default value inside the function if it is required in calculations. The output corresponds to the first two elements of the output list of `motion`.

2. **Without any output:** The output list can be omitted entirely if the computed quantities are not of any interest. This might be the case when the function displays the desired result graphically. To execute the function this way, just type the name of the function with the input list. For example, `motion(xt,yt,time);` will execute the function `motion` without generating any explicit output, provided that `xt`, `yt`, and `time` are defined, of course. If the semicolon at the end of the call statement is omitted, the first output variable in the output-list of the function is displayed in the default variable `ans`.

A function can be written to accept a partial list of inputs if some default value of the other unspecified inputs is defined inside the function. This kind of input list manipulation can be done with the built-in function `nargin`, which stands for number-of-arguments-in. Similarly, the list of output can be manipulated with the built-in function `nargout`. See on-line help on `nargin` and `nargout`. For an example, look at the function `fplot` by typing `type fplot.m`.

Example of a Simple Function File:

Let us write a function file to solve the same system of linear equations that we solved above in Section 4.1 using a script file. This time, we will make r an input to the function and *det_A* and x will be the outputs. Let us call this function **solvexf**. *As a rule, it must be saved in a file called* **solvexf.m**.

```
function [det_A, x] = solvexf(r);
% SOLVEXF solves a 3X3 matrix equation with parameter r
% This is the function file 'solvexf.m'
% To call this function, type:
%   [det_A,x] = solvexf(r);
% r is the input and det_A and x are output.
%_____

A = [5 2*r r; 3 6 2*r-1; 2 r-1 3*r]; % create matrix A
b = [2;3;5];                         % create vector b
det_A = det(A);                      % find the determinant
x = A\b;                             % find x.
```

Now r, x and *det_A* are all local variables. Therefore, any other variable names may be used in their places in the function call statement. Let us execute this function in MATLAB .

```
>> [detA, y] = solvexf(1);    % take r=1 and execute solvexf.m

>> detA                       % display the value of detA

ans =
      64

>> y                          % display the value of y

ans =
    -0.0312
     0.2344
     1.6875
```

Values of detA and y will be automatically displaced if the semi-colon at the end of the function execution command is omitted.

After execution of a function, the only variables left in the workspace by the function will be the variables in the output list. This gives us more control over input and output than we can get with script files. We can also put error checks and messages inside the function. For example, we could modify the function above to check if matrix A is empty or not and display an appropriate message before solving the system, by changing the last line to:

```
if isempty(A)                    % if matrix A is empty
    disp('Matrix A is empty');
else                             % if A is not empty
    x = A\b;                     % find x
end                              % end of if statement.
```

For a description of `if-elseif-else` branching and other control flow commands, see Section 4.4.4 on page 92.

4.2.2 More on functions

By now the difference between scripts and functions should be clear to you. The variables inside a function are local and are erased after execution of the function. But the variables inside a script file are left in the MATLAB workspace after execution of the script. Functions can have arguments, script files do not. What about functions inside another function? Are they local? How are they executed? Can a function be passed as an input variable to another function? Now we address these questions.

Executing a function inside another function

Usually, it is a straightforward process, so much that you do not have to pay any special attention to it. In the function `solvexf` above, we used a built-in function, `det`, to calculate the determinant of A. We used the function just the way we would use it on MATLAB prompt or in a script file. It is true for all functions, built-in or user-written. The story is different only when you want the function name to be *dynamic*, that is, if the function to be executed inside may be different with different executions of the calling function. [1] In such cases, the actual name of the function is passed to the calling function through the input list and a dummy name is used inside the calling function. The mechanism of passing the function name and evaluating it inside the calling function is quite different from that for a variable. We explain it below.

---

[1] A function that uses another function inside its body is called a *calling function* For example, `solvexf` in the example above is a calling function for the function `det`.

A function in the input list:

When a function needs to be passed in the input list of another function, the name of the function to be passed must appear as a character string in the input list. For example, the built-in function `fzero` finds a zero of a user-supplied function of a single variable. The call syntax of the function is `fzero(f,x)` where `f` is the name of the function and `x` is an initial guess. If we write a function `fr3` (saved as the file `fr3.m`) for solving, say, $f(r) = r^3 - 32.5r^2 + (r - 22)r + 100$, we may call `fzero` with the statements— `fzero('fr3',5)`. Note the single quotes around the name of the input function `fr3`.

Evaluating a function with `feval`

The function `feval` evaluates a function whose name is specified as a string at the given list of input variables. For example `[y, z] = feval ('Hfunction', x, t);` evaluates the function `Hfunction` on the input variables `x` and `t` and returns the output in `y` and `z`. It is equivalent to typing `[y, z] = Hfunction (x,t)`. So why would you ever evaluate a function using `feval` when you can evaluate the function directly? The most common use is when you want to evaluate functions with different names but the same input list. Consider the following situation. You want to evaluate any given function of x and y at the origin $x = 0$, $y = 0$. You can write a script file with one command in it:

`value = feval ('funxy', 0, 0);`

Now suppose Harry has a function $z(x, y) = \sin xy + xy^2$, programmed as:

```
function  z = harrysf(x,y)
% function to evaluate z(x,y)
z = sin(x*y)/exp(5*x) + x*y^2;
```

and Kelly has a function $h(x, y) = 20xy - 3y^3 - 2x^3 + 10$, programmed as

```
function  h = kellysf(x,y)
% function to evaluate h(x,y)
h = 20*x*y - 3*y^3 - 2*x^3 + 10;
```

Both functions can be evaluated with your script file by changing the name `funxy` to `harrysf` and `kellysf`, respectively. The point here is that the command in your script file takes *dynamic* filenames.

The use of feval becomes essential [2] when a function is passed as an input variable to another function. In such cases, the function passed as an input variable must be evaluated using **feval** inside the calling function. For example, the ODE (ordinary differential equation) solvers **ode23** and **ode45** take user-defined functions as inputs in which the user specifies the differential equation. Inside **ode23** and **ode45**, the user-defined function is evaluated at the current time t and the current value of x to compute the derivative $\dot{x}$ using **feval**. **ode23** and **ode45** are M-files, which you can copy and edit. Make a printout of one of them and see how it uses **feval**.

Writing good functions

Writing functions in MATLAB is easier than writing functions in most standard programming languages, or, for that matter, in most of the software packages that support their own programming environment. However, writing efficient and elegant functions is an art that comes only through experience. For starters, keeping the following points in mind helps.

- **Pseudo-code:** Before you begin writing the function, write a *pseudo-code*. It is essentially the entire function in plain English. Think about the logical structure and the sequence of computations, define the input and output variables, and write the function in plain words. Then begin the translation into MATLAB language.

- **Readability:** Select a sensible names for the function and the variables inside it. Write enough comments in the body of the function. Design and write helpful comments for on-line help (the comment lines in the beginning of the function). Make sure you include the syntax of how to use the function.

- **Modularity:** Keep your functions *modular*, that is, break big computations into smaller chunks and write separate functions for them. Keep your functions small in length.

- **Robustness:** Provide checks for errors and exit with helpful error messages.

- **Expandability:** Leave room for growth. For example, if you are writing a function with scalar variables, but you think you may use vector variables later, write the function this in mind. Avoid hardcoding actual numbers.

---

[2] unless you are comfortable with **eval** (see page 60) and can replace **feval(fun,x,y)** with **eval([fun,'(x,y)'])** where **fun** is a character string containing the name of the desired function.

4.3 Applications

4.3.1 Solving ordinary differential equations

*On-line
help
topic:*
ode23,
ode45

Ordinary Differential Equations (ODEs) are solved in MATLAB using the built-in
functions ode23 or ode45. These functions are implementations of 2nd/3rd-order
and 4th/5th-order Runge-Kutta methods, respectively. Solving ODEs using these
functions involves the following four steps:

1. **Write the differential equation(s) as a set of first-order ODEs.** For
   ODEs of order ≥ 2, this step involves introducing new variables and recasting
   the original equation(s) in terms of 1st-order ODEs in the new variables.

2. **Write a function to compute the new state derivative.** The state
   derivative is just the vector of derivatives of the new variables. If the system
   consists of more than one equation, put the variables of all the equations in
   the same state vector.

3. **Use the built-in ODE solvers ode23 or ode45 to solve the equations.**
   Your function written in Step-2 is used as an input to ode23 or ode45. The
   syntax of use of ode23 is shown below. To use ode45 just replace 'ode23' with
   'ode45'.

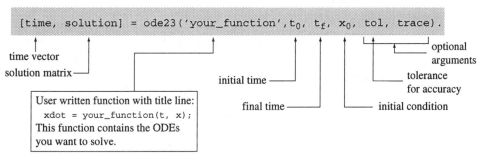

The *optional arguments*: tol specifies relative accuracy of the computed solution, and trace, if non-zero, shows some intermediate results.

4. **Extract the desired variables from the output and interpret the
   results.** For a system of n equations, the solution matrix solution contains n
   columns. You need to understand which column corresponds to which variable
   in order to extract the correct column, if you want to plot a variable with
   respect to, say, the independent variable time.

Here are two examples.

Example–1: A first-order linear ODE

Solve the first-order linear differential equation:

$$\frac{dx}{dt} = x + t \qquad\qquad (4.2)$$

with the initial condition

$$x(0) = 0.$$

Step-1: Write the equation(s) as a system of first-order equations: The given equation is already a first-order equation. No change is required.

$$\dot{x} = x + t.$$

Step-2: Write a function to compute the new derivatives: The function should return $\dot{x}$ given x and t. Here is the function:

```
function xdot = simpode(t,x);
% SIMPODE: computes xdot = x+t.
% call syntax:  xdot = simpode(t,x);
xdot = x + t;
```

Write and save it as an M-file named **simpode.m**.

Step-3: Use ode23 or ode45 to compute the solution: The commands as typed in the command window are shown below. These commands could instead be part of a script file or even another MATLAB function. Note that we have not used the optional arguments tol or trace.

```
>> ti = 0; tf = 2; x0 = 0;    % specify values of ti,tf and x0
>> [t,x] = ode23('simpode', ti, tf, x0);   % now execute ode23
```

Step-4: Extract and interpret results: The output variables t and x contain results— t is a vector containing all discrete points of time at which the solution was obtained, and x contains the values of the variable x at those instances of time. Let us see the solution graphically:

```
>> plot(t,x)                    % plot t vs x and label axes.
>> xlabel('t'), ylabel('x')     % put labels
```

The plot generated by above commands is shown in Figure 4.1.

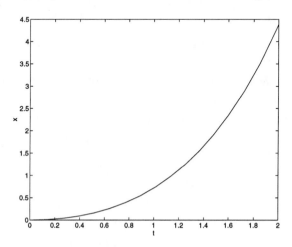

Figure 4.1: Numerical solution of $\dot{x} = x + t$ using ode23.

Example–2: A second-order nonlinear ODE:

Solve the equation of motion of a nonlinear pendulum:

$$\ddot{\theta} + \omega^2 \sin\theta = 0 \quad \Rightarrow \quad \ddot{\theta} = -\omega^2 \sin\theta \tag{4.3}$$

with the initial conditions

$$\theta(0) = 1, \quad \dot{\theta}(0) = 0.$$

Step-1: Write the equation(s) as a system of first-order equations: The given equation is a second-order ODE. To recast it as a system of two first-order equations (an nth-order equation reduces to a set of n 1st-order equations), let us introduce two new variables.

Let $z_1 = \theta$ and $z_2 = \dot{\theta}$. Then $\dot{z}_1 = \dot{\theta} = z_2$ and $\dot{z}_2 = \ddot{\theta} = -\omega^2 \sin(z_1)$. Now eqn. (4.3) may be written in vector form as:

$$\left\{ \begin{array}{c} \dot{z}_1 \\ \dot{z}_2 \end{array} \right\} = \left\{ \begin{array}{c} z_2 \\ -\omega^2 \sin(z_1) \end{array} \right\}$$

We may write this equation in vector form as

$$\dot{\mathbf{z}} = \mathbf{f}(\mathbf{z})$$

where $\dot{\mathbf{z}}, \mathbf{z}$ and $\mathbf{f}(\mathbf{z})$ are vectors with two components each:

$$\mathbf{z} = \left\{ \begin{array}{c} z_1 \\ z_2 \end{array} \right\}, \qquad \dot{\mathbf{z}} = \left\{ \begin{array}{c} \dot{z}_1 \\ \dot{z}_2 \end{array} \right\} = \left\{ \begin{array}{c} z_2 \\ -\omega^2 \sin z_1 \end{array} \right\} = \mathbf{f}(\mathbf{z}).$$

This is a special case of $\dot{\mathbf{z}} = \mathbf{f}(t, \mathbf{z})$ where $\mathbf{f}$ does not depend on t.

Step-2: Write a function to compute the new state derivative: We need to
write a function that, given the scalar time t and vector $\mathbf{z}$ as input, returns
the time derivative vector $\dot{\mathbf{z}}$ as output. In addition, the state derivative vector
$\dot{\mathbf{z}}$ must be a column vector. Here is a function that serves the purpose.

```
function zdot = pend(t,z);
% Call syntax: zdot = pend(t,z);
% Inputs are:  t = time
%              z = [z(1); z(2)] = [theta; thetadot]
% Output is :  zdot = [z(2); -w^2 sin z(1)]
wsq = 1.56;    % specify a value of w^2
zdot = [z(2); -wsq*sin(z(1))];
```

Note that $\mathbf{z}(1)$ and $\mathbf{z}(2)$ refer to the first and second elements of vector $\mathbf{z}$.
Do not forget to save the function 'pend' as an M-file to make it accessible to
MATLAB.

Step-3: Use ode23 or ode45 for solution: This time let us write a script file
that solves the system and plots the results. Remember that the output $\mathbf{z}$
contains two columns: z_1, which is actually θ, and z_2, which is $\dot{\theta}$. Here is
a script file that executes **ode23**, extracts the displacement and velocity in
vectors $\mathbf{x}$ and $\mathbf{y}$, and plots them against time as well as in the phase plane.

```
ti = 0; tf = 20; z0 = [1;0];        % assign values to ti, tf, z0.
[t,z] = ode23('pend',ti,tf,z0);     % run ode23
x = z(:,1); y = z(:,2);             % x = 1st column of z, y = 2nd column
plot(t,x,t,y)                       % plot time vs x and y on the same plot.
xlabel('t'), ylabel('x and y')
```

```
figure(2)                              % open a new figure window
plot(x,y)                              % plot phase portrait in the new window
xlabel('Displacement'), ylabel('Velocity')
title('Phase Plane of a Non-linear Pendulum')     % put a title
```

Step-4: Extract and interpret results: The desired variables have already been extracted and plotted by the script file in Step-3. The plots obtained are shown in Fig. 4.2 and Fig. 4.3.

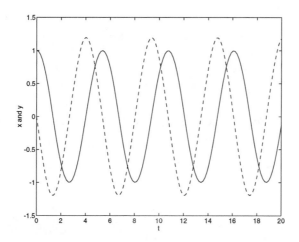

Figure 4.2: Displacement and velocity vs time plot of the pendulum.

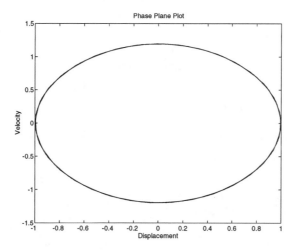

Figure 4.3: Displacement vs velocity plot of the pendulum.

4.3.2 Solving a nonlinear algebraic equation

The MATLAB function `fzero` solves nonlinear equations involving one variable. You can use `fzero` by proceeding with the following three steps.

1. **Write the equation in the standard form:**

$$f(x) = 0.$$

   This step usually involves trivial rearrangement of the given equation. In this form, solving the equation and *finding a zero of $f(x)$* are equivalent.

2. **Write a function that computes $f(x)$:** The function should return the value of $f(x)$ at any given x.

3. **Use the built-in function `fzero` to find the solution:** `fzero` requires an initial guess and returns the value of x closest to the guess at which $f(x)$ is zero. The function written in Step-2 is used as an input to the function `fzero`. The call syntax of `fzero` is:

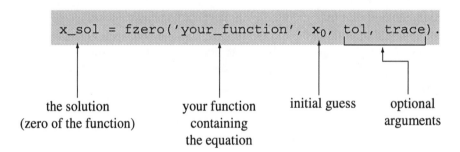

```
x_sol = fzero('your_function', x_0, tol, trace).
```

the solution (zero of the function)	your function containing the equation	initial guess	optional arguments

Example: A transcendental equation

Solve the following transcendental equation:

$$\sin x = e^x - 5.$$

Step-1: Write the equation in standard form: Rearrange the equation as

$$\sin(x) - e^x + 5 = 0 \Rightarrow \qquad f(x) = \sin(x) - e^x + 5.$$

Step-2: Write a function that computes $f(x)$: This is easy enough:

```
function f = transf(x);
% TRANSF: computes f(x) = sin(x)-exp(x)+5.
% call syntax:  f = transf(x);
f = sin(x) - exp(x) + 5;
```

Write and save the function as an M-file named **transf.m**.

Step-3: Use fzero to find the solution: The commands as typed in the command window are shown below. The result obtained is also shown. Note that we have not used the *optional arguments* tol or trace.

```
>> x = fzero('transf',1)          % initial guess x0=1.

x =

      1.7878
```

To check the result we can plug the value back into the equation or plot $f(x)$ and see if the answer looks right. See the plot of the function in Fig. 4.4.

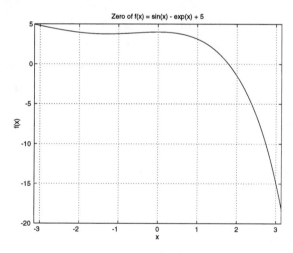

Figure 4.4: **fzero** locates the zero of this function at $x = 1.7878$.

You can also find the zeros of a polynomial equation (e.g., $x^5 - 3x^3 + x^2 - 9 = 0$) with **fzero**. However, **fzero** locates the root closest to the initial guess; it does not give all roots. To find all roots of a polynomial equation, use the built-in function **roots**. Finding multiple roots of a non-polynomial or finding roots of functions of several variables is a more advanced problem.

| On-line |
| help |
| category: |
| `lang` |

4.4   Language-Specific Features

We have already discussed numerous features of MATLAB's language through many examples in the previous sections. You are advised to pay special attention to proper usage of punctuation marks and different delimiters (page 155), and operators, especially the array operators (a period (.) preceding the arithmetic operators, page 52) and the relational operators (page 52). For control-flow, MATLAB provides `for` and `while` loops and an `if-elseif-else` construct. All the three control-flow statements must terminate with corresponding `end` statements. We now discuss flow control and some other specific features of the language. See on-line help for more details.

4.4.1   Use of comments to create on-line help

As we have already pointed out in the discussion on function files (page 77), the comment lines at the beginning (before any executable statement) of a script or a function file are used by MATLAB as on-line help on that file. This automatically creates on-line help for user-written functions. It is a good idea to copy the function definition line without the word `function` among those first few comment lines so that the execution syntax of the function is displayed by the on-line help. The command `lookfor` looks for the argument string in the first commented line of m-files. Therefore, in keeping with the somewhat confusing convention of MATLAB's built-in functions, you should write the name of the script or function file in uppercase letters followed by a short description with keywords, as the first commented line. Thus the first line following the function definition line in the example function on page 79 reads

```
% SOLVEXF solves a 3x3 matrix equation with parameter r.
```

4.4.2   Continuation

An ellipsis (three consecutive periods, '...') at the end of a line denotes continuation. So, if you type a command that does not fit on a single line, you may split it across two or more lines by using an ellipsis at the end of each but the last line. *Examples:*

```
A = [1 3 3 3; 5 10 -2 -20; 3 5 ...
        10 2; 1 0 0 9];
x = sin(linspace(1,6*pi,100)) .* cos(linspace(1,6*pi,100)) +...
        0.5*ones(1,100);
```

```
plot(tube_length,fluid_pressure,':',tube_length,...
     theoretical_pressure,'-')
```

You *may not*, however, use continuation inside a character string. For example, typing

```
logo = 'I am not only the President and CEO of Miracle Hair,...
        but also a client';
```

produces an error. For creating such long strings, break the string into smaller string segments and use concatenation (see Section 3.2.6).

4.4.3 Global variables

It is possible to declare a set of variables to be globally accessible to all or some functions without passing the variables in the input list. This is done with the global command. For example, the statement global x y z declares the variables x, y, and z to be global. This statement goes before any executable statement in the functions and scripts that need to access the values of the global variables. Be careful with the names of the global variables. It is generally a good idea to name such variables with long strings to avoid any unintended match with other local variables.

Example: Consider solving the following 1st-order ODE:

$$\dot{x} = kx + c\sin t, \qquad x(0) = 1.0$$

where you are interested in solutions for various values of k and c. Your script file may look like:

```
% scriptfile to solve a 1st-order ode.
t0 = 0;  tf = 20;              % specify initial and final time
x0 = 1.0;                      % specify initial condition
[t, x] = ode23 ('ode1',t0,x0); % execute ode23 to solve the ODE.
```

and the function 'ode1' may look like:

```
function xdot = ode1(t,x);
% ODE1: function to compute the derivative xdot
% at given t and x.
% Call syntax: xdot = ode1 (t,x);
% -------------
xdot = k*x + c*sin(t);
```

But this won't work.

In order for **ode1** to compute **xdot**, the values of k and c must be prescribed. These values could be prescribed inside the function **ode1** but you would have to edit this function each time you change the values of k and c. The alternative is to prescribe the values in the script file and make them available to the function **ode1** through *global* declaration.

```
% scriptfile to solve 1st-order ode.
global k_value c_value        % declare global variables
k_value = 5;  c_value = 2;    % specify the values of global variables
t0 = 0;  tf = 20;             % specify initial and final time
x0 = 1.0;                     % specify initial condition
[t, x] = ode23 ('ode1',t0,x0); % execute ode23 to solve the ODE.
```

Now you have to modify the function **ode1** so that it can access the global variables:

```
function xdot = ode1(t,x);
% ODE1: function to compute the derivative xdot
% at given t and x.
% Call syntax: xdot = ode1(t,x);
% -------------
global k_value c_value
xdot = k_value*x + c_value*sin(t)
```

Now, if the values of **k_value** and **c_value** are changed in the script file, the new values become available to **ode1** too. Note that the global declaration is only in the script file and the user function file **ode1**, and therefore **k_value** and **c_value** will be available to these files only.

On-line help category: `lang`

4.4.4   Loops, branches, and control-flow

MATLAB has its own syntax for control-flow statements like *for*-loops, *while*-loops and, of course, *if-elseif-else* branching. In addition, it provides three commands— **break, error,** and **return** to control the execution of scripts and functions. A description of these functions follows.

For loops:

A **for** loop is used to repeat a statement or a group of statements for a fixed number of times. Here are two examples:

Example-1:
```
for m=1:100
    num = 1/(m+1)
end
```
Example-2:
```
for n=100:-2:0, k = 1/(exp(m)), end
```

The *counter* in the loop can also be given explicit increment: `for i=m:k:n` to advance the counter `i` by `k` each time (in the second example above `n` goes from 100 to 0 as 100, 98, 96, ..., etc.). You can have nested `for`-loops, that is, `for`-loops within `for`-loops. *Every* `for`, *however, must be matched with an* `end`.

While loops:

A `while` loop is used to execute a statement or a group of statements for an indefinite number of times until the condition specified by `while` is no longer satisfied. For example:

```
% let us find all powers of 2 below 10000
v = 1;   i=1;
while num < 10000
       num = 2^i;
       v = [v; num];
       i = i + 1;
end
```

Once again, a `while` must have a matching `end`.

If-elseif-else statements:

This construction provides a logical branching for computations. An example is:

```
if i > 5
   do something
elseif (i>1) & (j==20)
   do this
else
   do that
end
```

Of course, you can have nested `if` statements, as long as you have matching `end` statements. You can nest all three kinds of loops, in any combination.

Break

The command **break** inside a **for** or **while** loop terminates the execution of the loop, even if the condition for execution of the loop is true.

Examples:

1.
```
for i=1:length(v)
     if u(i) < 0          % check for negative u
        break             % terminate loop execution
     end
     a = v(i) + .....  % do something
 end
```

2.
```
while 1
     n = input('Enter max. number of iterations ')
     if n <= 0
        break             % terminate loop execution
     end
     for i=1:n
        .....             % do something
     end
 end
```

If the loops are nested then **break** terminates only the innermost loop.

Error

The command **error(**'*message*'**)** inside a function or a script aborts the execution, displays the error message *message*, and returns the control to the keyboard.

Example:

```
function c = crossprod(a,b);
% crossprod(a,b) calculates the cross product axb.
if nargin~=2           % if not two input arguments
   error('Sorry, need two input vectors')
end
if length(a)==2        % begin calculations
   ....
end
```

Return

The command `return` simply returns the control to the invoking function. *Example:*

```
function animatebar(t0,tf,x0);
% animatebar animates a bar pendulum.
   :
disp('Do you want to see the phase portrait?')
ans = input('Enter 1 if YES, 0 if NO '); % see below for description
if ans==0                  % if the input is 0
   return                  % exit function
else
   plot(x,...)             % show the phase plot
end
```

4.4.5 Interactive input

On-line help category: `lang`

The commands—`input`, `keyboard`, `menu`, and `pause` can be used inside a script or a function file for interactive user input. Their descriptions follow.

Input

The command `input('`*string*`')`, used in the previous example, displays the text in *string* on the screen and waits for the user to give keyboard input.

Examples:

- `n = input('Largest square matrix size ');` prompts the user to input the the size of the 'largest square matrix' and saves the input in `n`.

- `more = input('More simulations?  (Y/N) ','s');` prompts the user to type `Y` for YES and `N` for NO and stores the input as a string in `more`. Note that the second argument, `'s'`, of the command directs MATLAB to save the user input as a string.

This command can be used to write *user-friendly* interactive programs in MATLAB.

Keyboard

The command `keyboard` inside a script or a function file returns control to the keyboard at the point where the command occurs. The execution of the function or the script is *not* terminated. The command window prompt ≫ changes to k≫ to show the special status. At this point, you can check variables already computed, change their values, and issue any valid MATLAB commands. The control is returned to the function by typing the word **return** on the special prompt k≫ and then pressing the return key.

This command is useful for debugging functions. Sometimes, in long computations, you may like to check some intermediate results, plot them and see if the computation is headed in the right direction, and then let the execution continue.

Example:

```
%---- RunRobot: a script file for robotics computation -----
% This file calls a few other functions.
datascript               % script file that reads input data
[x,y,z,P] = position(n,q);
keyboard                 % invoke keyboard to check some stuff
[finalp,angles] = robot(x,y,z,P);
plotscript               % script file for plotting things
```

During the execution of the above script file **RunRobot.m**, the control is returned to the keyboard just after the execution of the function **position**. The execution of **RunRobot** resumes after the control is returned to the script file by typing **return** on the special prompt k≫ .

Menu

The command **menu**(*'MenuName','option1','option2',..*) creates an on-screen menu with the *MenuName* and lists the options in the menu. The user can select any of the options using the mouse or the keyboard depending on the computer. The implementation of this command on Macs and PCs creates nice window menu with buttons.

Example:

```
% Plotting a circle
r = input('Enter the desired radius ');
theta = linspace(0,2*pi,100);
r = r*ones(size(theta));    % make r the same size as theta
coord = menu('Circle Plot','Cartesian','Polar');
if coord==1                 % if the first option is selected
                            %- from the menu
    plot(r.*cos(theta),r.*sin(theta))
    axis('square')
else                        % if the second option is selected
                            %- from the menu
    polar(theta,r);
end
```

In the above script file, the **menu** command creates a menu with the name Circle Plot and two options—Cartesian and Polar. The options are internally numbered. When the user selects one of the options, the corresponding number is passed on to the variable **coord**. The **if-else** structure following the **menu** command shows what to do with each option. Try out this script file.

Pause

The command **pause** temporarily halts the current process. It can be used with or without an optional argument:

pause   halts the current process and waits for the user to give 'go-ahead' signal. Pressing any key resumes the process.

   Example: for i=1:n, plot(X(:,i),Y(:,i)), pause, end.

pause(n) halts the current process, pauses for n seconds, and then resumes the process.

   Example: for i=1:n, plot(X(:,i),Y(:,i)), pause(5), end

              pauses for 5 seconds before it plots the next graph.

4.4.6   Recursion

The MATLAB programming language supports recursion, i.e., a function can call itself during its execution. Thus recursive algorithms can be directly implemented in MATLAB (what a break for Fortran users!).

4.4.7   Input/output

MATLAB supports many standard C-language file I/O functions for reading and writing formatted binary and text files. The functions supported include:

On-line help category: iofun

fopen	opens an existing file or creates a new file
fclose	closes an open file
fread	reads binary data from a file
fwrite	writes binary data to a file
fscanf	reads formatted data from a file
fprintf	writes formatted data to a file
sscanf	reads strings in specified format
sprintf	writes data in formatted string
fgets	reads a line from file discarding new-line character
fgetl	reads a line from file including new-line character
frewind	rewinds a file
fseek	sets the file position indicator
ftell	gets the current file position indicator
ferror	inquires file I/O error status.

You are likely to use only the first six commands in the list for file I/O. For most purposes fopen, fprintf, and fclose should suffice. For a complete description of these commands see on-line help or consult the Reference Guide [2] or a C-language reference book[6].

Here is a simple example that uses fopen, fprintf, and fclose to create and write formatted data to a file:

```
% TEMTABLE - generates and writes a temperaure table
% Script file to generate a Fahrenheit-Celcius
% temperature table. The table is written in
% a file named 'Temperature.table'.
% ---------------------------------------------------
F=-20:5:70;             % take F=[-20 -15 -10 .. 70]
C=(f-32)*5/9;           % compute corresponding C
t=[F;C];                % create a matrix t (2 rows)
fid = fopen('Temperature.table','w');
fprintf(fid,'  Temperature Table\n ');
fprintf(fid,' ~~~~~~~~~~~~~~~~ \n');
fprintf(fid,'Fahrenheit    Celsius \n');
fprintf(fid,' %4i      %8.2f\n',t);
fclose(fid);
```

In the above script file, the first I/O command, fopen, opens a file Temperature.table in the *write* mode (specified by 'w' in the command) and assigns the *file identifier* to fid. The following fprintf commands use fid to write the strings and data to that file. The data is formatted according to the specifications in the string argument of fprintf. In the command above, \n stands for *new line*, %4i stands for an *integer* field of width 4, and %8.2f stands for a *fixed point* field of width 8 with 2 digits after the decimal point.

The output file, Temperature.table, is shown below:

```
Temperature Table
~~~~~~~~~~~~~~~~~~
Fahrenheit    Celsius
   -40        -40.00
   -35        -37.22
   -30        -34.44
   -25        -31.67
   -20        -28.89
   -15        -26.11
   -10        -23.33
    -5        -20.56
     0        -17.78
     5        -15.00
    10        -12.22
    15         -9.44
    20         -6.67
    25         -3.89
    30         -1.11
    35          1.67
    40          4.44
    45          7.22
    50         10.00
    55         12.78
    60         15.56
    65         18.33
    70         21.11
    75         23.89
    80         26.67
    85         29.44
    90         32.22
    95         35.00
   100         37.78
```

5. *Graphics*

MATLAB 4.x includes good tools for visualization. Basic 2-D plots, fancy 3-D graphics with lighting and color-maps, complete user-control of the graphics objects through *Handle Graphics*, tools for design of sophisticated graphics user-interface, and animation are now part of MATLAB. What is special about MATLAB's graphics facility is its ease of use and expandability. Commands for most garden-variety plotting are simple, easy to use, and intuitive. If you are not satisfied with what you get, you can control and manipulate virtually everything in the graphics window. This, however, requires an understanding of the Handle Graphics, a system of low-level functions to manipulate graphics objects. In this section we take you through the main features of the MATLAB's graphics facilities.

5.1 Basic 2-D Plots

On-line help category: plotxy

The most basic and perhaps the most useful command for producing a simple 2-D plot is

$$\texttt{plot}(xvalues,\ yvalues,\ 'style\text{-}option')$$

where *xvalues* and *yvalues* are vectors containing the *x*- and *y*-coordinates of points on the graph and the *style-option* is an optional argument that specifies the line or the point style (e.g. solid, dashed, dotted, o, +, etc.) and the color of the line to be plotted. The two vectors *xvalues* and *yvalues* MUST have the same length. Unequal length of the two vectors is the most common source of error in the plot command. The `plot` function also works with a single vector argument, in which case the elements of the vector are plotted against row or column indices. Thus, for two column vectors x and y each of length n,

`plot(x,y)`	plots y vs. x with a solid line (the default line style),
`plot(x,y,'--')`	plots y vs. x with a dashed line (more on this below),
`plot(x)`	plots the elements of x against their row index.

5.1.1   Line-style options

The *style-option* in the plot command is a character string that consists of 1, 2, or 3 characters that specify the color and/or the line style. There are eight color options and nine line-style options:

Color Style-option		Line Style-option	
y	yellow	−	solid
m	magenta	--	dashed
c	cyan	:	dotted
r	red	-.	dash-dot
g	green	.	point
b	blue	o	circle
w	white	x	x-mark
k	black	+	plus
		*	star

The *style-option* is made up of either the color option, the line-style option, or a combination of the two.

Examples:

`plot(x,y,'r')`	plots y vs. x with a red solid line,
`plot(x,y,':')`	plots y vs. x with a dotted line,
`plot(x,y,'b--')`	plots y vs. x with a blue dashed line,
`plot(x,y,'+')`	plots y vs. x as unconnected discrete points marked by +.

When no style option is specified, MATLAB uses the default option—a yellow solid line.

-line

)

gory:

phics

5.1.2   Labels, title, legend, and other text objects

Plots may be annotated with `xlabel`, `ylabel`, `title`, and `text` commands.
The first three commands take string arguments, while the last one requires three
arguments— `text`(*x-coordinate, y-coordinate, 'text'*), where the coordinate values
are taken from the current plot. Thus,

`xlabel('Pipe Length')`	labels the x-axis with `Pipe Length`,
`ylabel('Fluid Pressure')`	labels the y-axis with `Fluid Pressure`,
`title('Pressure Variation Study')`	titles the plot with `Pressure Variation Study`,
`text(2,6,'Note this dip')`	writes 'Note this dip' at the location (2.0,6.0) in the current plot coordinates.

We have already seen an example of `xlabel`, `ylabel`, `and title` in Fig. 3.10.
An example of `text` appears in Fig. 5.1. The arguments of `text`(*x,y,'text'*) command may be vectors, in which case x and y must have the same length and *text*
may be just one string or a vector of strings. If *text* is a vector then it must have
the same length as x and, of course, like any other string vector, must have each
element of the same length. A useful variant of the `text` command is `gtext` , which
only takes string argument (a single string or a vector of strings) and lets the user
specify the location of the text by clicking the mouse at the desired location in the
graphics window.

Legend:

The `legend` command produces a boxed legend on a plot, as shown, for example,
in Fig. 5.2 on page 108. The `legend` command is quite versatile. It can take several
optional arguments. The most commonly used forms of the command are listed
below.

`legend(`*string1, string2, ..*`)`	produces legend using the text in *string1, string2, ..* as labels.
`legend(`*LineStyle1, string1, ..*`)`	specifies the line-style of each label.
`legend(..,` *tol*`)`	writes the legend outside the plot-frame if $tol = -1$ and inside the frame if $tol = 0$.
`legend off`	deletes the legend from the plot.

When MATLAB is asked to produce a legend, it tries to find a place on the plot where it can write the specified legend without running into lines, grid, and other graphics objects. The optional argument *tol* specifies the tolerance in terms of number of data points that may be covered by the legend. When the legend cannot be written within the specified tolerance, MATLAB writes the legend outside the plot. The user, however, can move the legend at will with the mouse (click and drag). For more information, see the on-line help by typing `help legend`.

5.1.3   Axis control, zoom-in, and zoom-out

Once a plot is generated you can change the axes limits with the `axis` command. Typing

$$\boxed{\texttt{axis([\textit{xmin xmax ymin ymax}])}}$$

changes the current axes limits to the specified new values *xmin* and *xmax* for the x-axis and *ymin* and *ymax* for the y-axis.

Examples:

`axis([-5 10 2 22]);`   sets the x-axis from -5 to 10 and the y-axis from 2 to 22.
`axy = [-5 10 2 22]; axis(axy);`   same as above.
`ax = [-5 10]; ay = [2 22]; axis([ax ay]);`   same as above.

The `axis` command may thus be used to zoom-in on a particular section of the plot or to zoom-out. [1] There are also some useful predefined string arguments for the `axis` command:

`axis('equal')`	sets equal scale on both axes
`axis('square')`	sets the default rectangular frame to a square
`axis('normal')`	resets the axis to default values
`axis('axis')`	freezes the current axes limits
`axis('off')`	removes the surrounding frame and the tick marks.

The `axis` command must come after the `plot` command to have the desired effect.

---

[1]There is also a `zoom` command which can be used to zoom-in and zoom-out using the mouse in the figure window. See on-line help on `zoom`

Semi-control of axes

It is possible to control only part of the axes limits and let MATLAB set the other limits automatically. This is achieved by specifying the desired limits in the `axis` command along with `inf` as the values of the limits which you would like to be set automatically. For example,

`axis([-5 10 -inf inf])`   sets the x-axis limits at -5 and 10 and lets the y-axis limits to be set automatically.

`axis([-5 inf -inf 22])`   sets the lower limit of the x-axis and the upper limit of the y-axis, and lets the two other limits to be set automatically.

5.1.4   Overlay plots

There are three different ways of generating overlay plots in MATLAB: the `plot`, `hold`, and `line` commands.

Method-1: Using the `plot` command to generate overlay plots

If the entire set of data is available, `plot` command with multiple arguments may be used to generate an overlay plot. For example, if we have three sets of data— (x1,y1), (x2,y2), and (x3,y3)—the command `plot(x1,y1, x2,y2,':', x3,y3,'o')` plots (x1,y1) with a solid line, (x2,y2) with a dotted line, and (x3,y3) as unconnected points marked by small circles ('o'), all on the same graph (See Fig. 5.1 for example). Note that the vectors (xi,yi) must have the same length pairwise. If the length of all vectors is the same then it might be more convenient to make a matrix of x vectors and a matrix of y vectors and then use the two matrices as the argument of the `plot` command. For example, if x1, y1, x2, y2, x3, and y3 are all column vectors of length n then typing `X=[x1 x2 x3]; Y=[y1 y2 y3]; plot(X,Y)` produces a plot with three lines drawn in different colors. When `plot` command is used with matrix arguments, each column of the second argument matrix is plotted against the corresponding column of the first argument matrix.

```
>>t=linspace(0,2*pi,100);          % Generate vector x
>>y1=sin(t); y2=t;                 % Calculate y1, y2, y3
>>y3=t-(t.^3)/6+(t.^5)/120;
>>plot(x,y1,x,y2,'--',x,y3,':')    % Plot (x,y1) with solid line
                                   %- (x,y2) with dahed line and
                                   %- (x,y3) with dotted line
>>axis([0 5 -1 5])                 % Zoom-in with new axis limits
>>xlabel('t')                      % Put x-label
>>ylabel('Approximations of sin(t)')% Put y-label
>>title('Fun with sin(t)')         % Put title
>>text(3.5,0,'sin(t)')             % Write 'sin(t)' at point (3.5,0)
>>gtext('Linear approximation')
>>gtext('First 3 terms')
>>gtext('in Taylor series')
```

gtext writes the specified string at a location clicked with the mouse in the graphics window. So after hitting return at the end of gtext command, go to the graphics window and click a location.

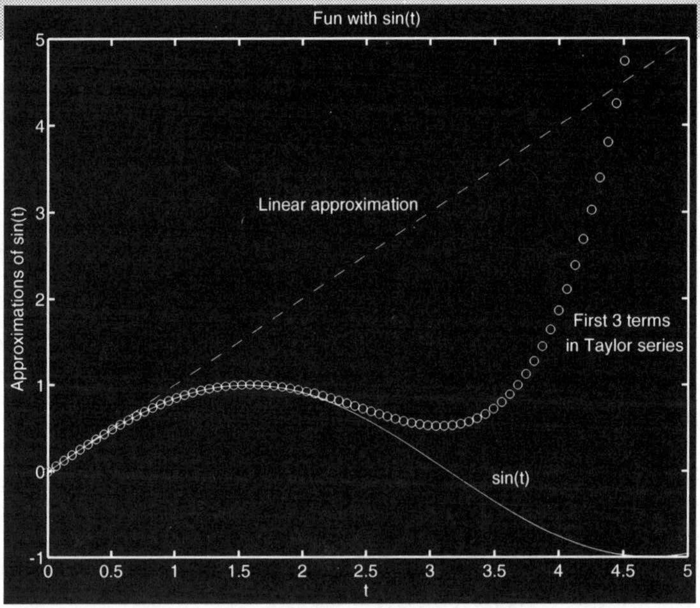

Figure 5.1: Example of an overlay plot along with examples of xlabel, ylabel, title, axis, text, and gtext commands. The three lines plotted are $y_1 = \sin t$, $y_2 = t$, and $y_3 = t - \frac{t^3}{3!} + \frac{t^5}{5!}$.

Method-2: Using the `hold` command to generate overlay plots

Another way of making overlay plots is with the `hold` command. Invoking `hold on` at any point during a session freezes the current plot in the graphics window. All subsequent plots generated by the `plot` command are simply added to the existing plot. The following script file shows how to generate the same plot as in Fig. 5.1 by using the `hold` command.

```
% ------ Script file to generate an overlay plot with the hold  command----
x=linspace(0,2*pi,100);          % Generate vector x
y1=sin(x);                       % Calculate y1
plot(x,y1)                       % Plot (x,y1) with solid line
hold on                          % Invoke hold for overlay plots
y2=x; plot(x,y2,'--')            % Plot (x,y2) with dashed line
y3=t-(t.^3)/6+(t.^5)/120;        % Calculate y3
plot(x,y3,'o')                   % Plot (x,y3) as pts. marked by 'o'

axis([0 5 -1 5])                 % Zoom-in with new axis limits
hold off                         % Clear hold command
```

The `hold` command is useful for overlay plots when the entire data set to be plotted is not available at the same time. You should use this command if you want to keep adding plots as the data becomes available. For example, if a set of calculations done in a `for` loop generates vectors x and y at the end of each loop and you would like to plot them on the same graph, `hold` is the way to do it.

Method-3: Using the `line` command to generate overlay plots

The `line` is a low-level graphics command which is used by the `plot` command to generate lines. Once a plot exists in the graphics window, additional lines may be added by using the `line` command directly. The `line` command takes a pair of vectors (or a triplet in 3-D) followed by *parameter name/parameter value* pairs as arguments:

> line(*xdata, ydata, ParameterName, ParameterValue*)

This command simply adds lines to the existing axes. For example, the overlay plot created by the above script file could also be created with the following script file, which uses the `line` command instead of the `hold` command. As a bonus to the reader, we include an example of the `legend` command (see page 103).

```
% ---- Script file to generate an overlay plot with the line command ----
t=linspace(0,2*pi,100);              % Generate vector t
y1=sin(t);                           % Calculate y1, y2, y3
y2=t;
y3=t-(t.^3)/6+(t.^5)/120;
plot(t,y1)                           % Plot (t,y1) with (default) solid line
line(t,y2,'linestyle','--')          % Add line (t,y2) with dahed line and
line(t,y3,'linestyle','o')           % Add line (t,y3) plotted with circles
axis([0 5 -1 5])                     % Zoom-in with new axis limits
xlabel('t')                          % Put x-label
ylabel('Approximations of sin(t)')
                                     % Put y-label
title('Fun with sin(t)')            % Put title
legend('sin(t)','linear approx.','5th order approx.')
                                     % add legend
```

The output generated by the above script file is shown in Fig. 5.2. After generating the plot, click and hold the mouse on the legend rectangle and see if you can drag the legend to some other position.

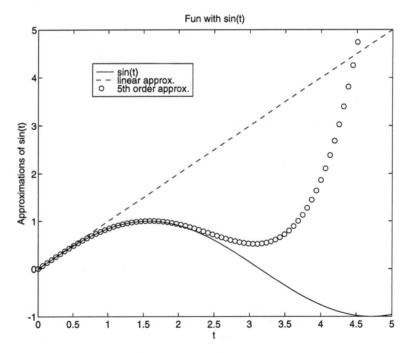

Figure 5.2: Example of an overlay plot produced by using the `line` command. The legend is produced by the `legend` command. See the script file for details.

5.1.5   Specialized 2-D plots

There are many specialized graphics functions for 2-D plotting. They are used as alternatives to the `plot` command we have just discussed. Here is an alphabetical list of the possible ways of plotting *x-y* data:

> *On-line help category:* `plotxy`

`bar`	creates a bar graph
`comet`	makes an animated 2-D plot
`compass`	creates arrow graph for complex numbers
`contour`	makes contour plots
`errorbar`	plots a graph and puts error bars
`fill`	draws filled polygons of specified color
`fplot`	plots a function of a single variable
`hist`	makes histograms
`loglog`	creates plot with log scale on both x and y axes
`pcolor`	makes pseudocolor plot of a matrix
`polar`	plots curves in polar coordinates
`quiver`	plots vector fields
`rose`	makes angled histograms
`semilogx`	makes semilog plot with log scale on the x-axis
`semilogy`	makes semilog plot with log scale on the y-axis
`stair`	plots a stair graph
`stem`	plots a stem graph

On the following pages we show examples of these functions. The commands shown in the middle column produce the plots shown in the right column. There are several ways you can use these graphics functions. Also, many of them take optional arguments. The following examples should give you a basic idea of how to use these functions and what kind of plot to expect from them. For more information on any of these functions see on-line help.

Function	Example Script	Output
fplot	$f(t) = t\sin t, \ 0 \le t \le 10\pi$ `fplot('x.*sin(x)',[0 10*pi])` Note that the function to be plotted must be written as a function of x.	

semilogx	$x = e^{-t}, \ y = t, \ 0 \le t \le 2\pi$
	
	 `t=linspace(0,2*pi,200);`
	 `x = exp(-t); y = t;`
	 `semilogx(x,y), grid`	

semilogy	$x = t, \ y = e^t, \ 0 \le t \le 2\pi$
	
	 `t=linspace(0,2*pi,200);`
	 `semilogy(t,exp(t))`
	 `grid`	

loglog	$x = e^t, \ y = 100 + e^{2t}, \ 0 \le t \le 2\pi$
	
	 `t=linspace(0,2*pi,200);`
	 `x = exp(t);`
	 `y = 100+exp(2*t);`
	 `loglog(x,y), grid`	

Function	Example Script	Output

polar	$r^2 = 2\sin 5t, \ \ 0 \le t \le 2\pi$
	
	 ```t=linspace(0,2*pi,200);```
	```r=sqrt(abs(2*sin(5*t)));```
	```polar(t,r)```	

fill	$\begin{aligned} r^2 &= 2\sin 5t, \ \ 0 \le t \le 2\pi \\ x &= r\cos t, \ \ y = r\sin t \end{aligned}$
	
	 ```t=linspace(0,2*pi,200);```
	```r=sqrt(abs(2*sin(5*t)));```
	```x=r.*cos(t);```
	```y=r.*sin(t);```
	```fill(x,y,'k'),```
	```axis('square')```	

bar	$\begin{aligned} r^2 &= 2\sin 5t, \ \ 0 \le t \le 2\pi \\ y &= r\sin t \end{aligned}$
	
	 ```t=linspace(0,2*pi,200);```
	```r=sqrt(abs(2*sin(5*t)));```
	```y=r.*sin(t);```
	```bar(t,y)```
	```axis([0 pi 0 inf]);```	

errorbar	$\begin{aligned} f_{\text{approx}} &= x - \frac{x^3}{3!}, \ \ 0 \le x \le 2 \\ error &= f_{\text{approx}} - \sin x \end{aligned}$
	
	 ```x=0:.1:2;```
	```aprx2=x-x.^3/6;```
	```er=aprx2-sin(x);```
	```errorbar(x,aprx2,er)```	

Function	Example Script	Output
| hist | Histogram of 50 randomly distributed numbers between 0 and 1.<br><br>```
y=randn(50,1);
hist(y)
``` | |
| stem | $f = e^{-t/5}\sin t,\ 0 \le t \le 2\pi$<br><br>```
t=linspace(0,2*pi,200);
f=exp(-.2*t).*sin(t);
stem(t,f)
``` | |
| stairs | $\begin{aligned} r^2 &= 2\sin 5t,\ \ 0 \le t \le 2\pi \\ y &= r\sin t \end{aligned}$<br><br>```
t=linspace(0,2*pi,200);
r=sqrt(abs(2*sin(5*t)));
y=r.*sin(t);
stairs(t,y)
axis([0 pi 0 inf]);
``` | |
| compass | $z = \cos\theta + i\sin\theta,\ \ -\pi \le \theta \le \pi$<br><br>```
th=-pi:pi/5:pi;
zx=cos(ts);
zy=sin(ts);
z=zx+i*zy;
compass(z)
``` | |

Function	Example Script	Output

comet	$y = t\sin t,\ \ 0 \le t \le 10\pi$
	
	`q=linspace(0,10*pi,200);`
	`y = q.*sin(q);`
	`comet(q,y)`
	(Its better to see it on screen)	

contour	$z = \dfrac{1}{2}x^2 + xy + y^2$
	 $|x| \le 5, |y| \le 5.$
	
	`r=-5:.2:5;`
	`[X,Y]=meshgrid(r,r);`
	`Z=.5*X.^2 + X.*Y + Y.^2;`
	`cs=contour(Z);`
	`clabel(cs)`	

quiver	$z = x^2 + y^2 - 5\sin(xy)$
	 $|x| \le 2, |y| \le 2.$
	
	`r=-2:.2:2;`
	`[X,Y]=meshgrid(r,r);`
	`Z=X.^2 -5*sin(X.*Y) + Y.^2;`
	`[dx,dy]=gradient(Z,.2,.2);`
	`quiver(X,Y,dx,dy,2);`	

pcolor	$z = x^2 + y^2 - 5\sin(xy)$
	 $|x| \le 2, |y| \le 2.$
	
	`r=-2:.2:2;`
	`[X,Y]=meshgrid(r,r);`
	`Z=X.^2 -5*sin(X.*Y) + Y.^2;`
	`pcolor(Z), axis('off')`
	`shading interp`	

5.2 Using subplot to Layout Multiple Graphs

If you want to make a few plots and place the plots side-by-side (not overlay), use the subplot command to design your layout. The subplot command requires three integer arguments:

$$\boxed{\texttt{subplot(m,n,p)}}$$

Subplot divides the graphics window into $m \times n$ sub-windows and puts the plot generated by the next plotting command into the pth sub-window where the sub-windows are counted row-wise. Thus, the command subplot(2,2,3), plot(x,y) divides the graphics window into 4 sub-windows and plots y vs. x in the 3rd sub-window, which is the first sub-window in the second row. See Fig. 5.4.

On-line
help
category:
plotxyz

5.3 3-D Plots

MATLAB 4.x provides extensive facilities for visualization of 3-D data. In fact, the built-in *colormaps* may be used to represent the 4th dimension. The facilities provided include built-in functions for plotting space-curves, wire-frame objects, surfaces, and shaded surfaces, generating contours automatically, specifying light sources, interpolating colors and shading, and even displaying images. Typing help plotxyz in the command window gives a list of functions available for general 3-D graphics. A list of commonly used functions follows.

plot3	plots curves in space
comet3	makes animated 3-D line plot
fill3	draws filled 3-D polygons
contour3	makes 3-D contour plots
mesh	draws 3-D mesh surfaces (wire-frame)
meshc	draws 3-D mesh surface along with contours
meshz	draws 3-D mesh surface with curtain plot of reference planes
surf	creates 3-D surface plots
surfc	creates 3-D surface plots along with contours
surfl	creates 3-D surface plots with specified light source
slice	draws a volumetric surface with slices
waterfall	creates a *waterfall* plot of 3-D data
cylinder	generates a cylinder
sphere	generates a sphere

Among these functions, `plot3` and `comet3` are the 3-D analogues of `plot` and `comet` commands mentioned in the 2-D graphics section. The general syntax for the `plot3` command is

plot3(*x, y, z, 'style-option'*)

This command plots a curve in 3-D space with the specified line style. The argument list can be repeated to make overlay plots, just the same way as with the `plot` command. A catalog of these functions with example scripts and the corresponding output is given on pages 122–125. Since the example scripts use a few functions which we have not discussed yet, we postpone the catalog till we discuss these functions.

Plots in 3-D may be annotated with functions already mentioned for 2-D plots—`xlabel`, `ylabel`, `title`, `text`, `gtext`, `grid`, etc., along with the obvious addition `zlabel`. The `grid` command in 3-D makes the 3-D appearance of the plots better, especially for curves in space (see Fig. 5.4 for example).

5.3.1 View

The viewing angle of the observer is specified by the command

view(*azimuth, elevation*)

where *azimuth*, in degrees, specifies the horizontal rotation from the y-axis, measured positive counterclockwise, and *elevation*, in degrees, specifies the vertical angle measured positive above the xy-plane (see Fig. 5.3). The default values for these angles are $-37.5°$ and $30°$ respectively.

By specifying appropriate values of the azimuth and the elevation, one can plot the projections of a three-dimensional object on different 2-D planes. For example, the command `view(90,0)` puts the viewer on the positive x-axis, looking straight on the yz-plane, and thus produces a 2-D projection of the object on the yz-plane. Figure 5.4 shows the projections obtained by specifying view angles. The script file used to generate the data, plot the curves, and obtain the different projected views is listed below.

```
%------ Script file with examples of 'subplot' and 'view' commands  -----
clg                         % Clear any previous graph
t=linspace(0,6*pi,100);     % Generate vector t with 100
                            %- equally spaced points between 0 and  6*pi
x=cos(t); y=sin(t); z=t;    % Calculate x, y, and z
```

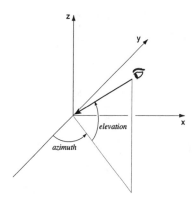

Figure 5.3: The viewing angles *azimuth* and *elevation* in 3-D plots.

```
subplot(2,2,1)                % Divide the graphics window into 4
                              %- subwindows and plot in the first  window
plot3(x,y,z),grid             % Plot the space curve in 3-D and put  grid
xlabel('cos(t)'),ylabel('sin(t)'),zlabel('t')
title('A circular helix: x(t)=cos(t), y(t)=sin(t), z(t)=t')

subplot(2,2,2),
plot3(x,y,z),  view(0,90),   % View along the z-axis from above
xlabel('cos(t)'),ylabel('sin(t)'),zlabel('t')
title('Projection in the X-Y plane')

subplot(2,2,3),
plot3(x,y,z),  view(0,0),     % View along the y-axis
xlabel('cos(t)'),ylabel('sin(t)'),zlabel('t')
title('Projection in the X-Z plane')

subplot(2,2,4),
plot3(x,y,z),  view(90,0),    % View along the x-axis
xlabel('cos(t)'),ylabel('sin(t)'),zlabel('t')
title('Projection in the Y-Z plane')
```

View(2) and View(3)

These are the special cases of the `view` command, specifying the default 2-D and 3-D views:

`view(2)`   same as `view(0,90)`, shows the projection in the xz-plane.

`view(3)`   same as `view(-37.5,30)`, shows the default 3-D view.

The `view(3)` command can be used to see a 2-D object in 3-D. It may be useful in visualizing the perspectives of different geometrical shapes. The following script

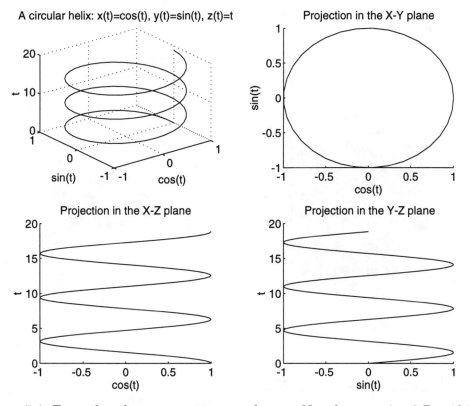

Figure 5.4: Examples of `plot3`, `subplot` and `view`. Note how putting 3-D grid in the background helps in the 3-D appearance of the space curve. Although the three 2-D pictures could be made using the `plot` command, this example illustrates the use of viewing angles.

file draws a filled circle in 2-D and also views the same circle in 3-D. The output is shown in Fig. 5.5

```
% ------- script file to draw a filled circle and view in 3D -----
theta = linspace(0,2*pi,100);    % create vector theta
x = cos(theta);                  % generate x-coordinates
y = sin(theta);                  % generate y-coordinates
subplot(1,2,1)                   % initiate a 1 by 2 subplot
fill(x,y,'g');axis('square');    % plot the filled circle
subplot(1,2,2)                   % go to the 2nd subplot
fill(x,y,'g');axis('square');    % plot the same circle again
view(3)                          % view the 2-D circle in 3-D
```

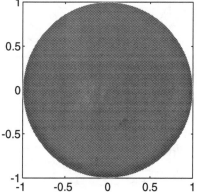 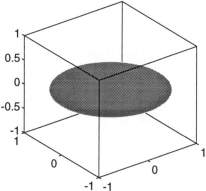

Figure 5.5: Example of view(3) to see a 2-D object in 3-D.

5.3.2   Mesh and surface plots

The functions for plotting meshes and surfaces mesh and surf, and their various variants meshz, meshc, surfc, and surfl, take multiple optional arguments, the most basic form being mesh(Z) or surf(Z), where Z represents a matrix. Usually surfaces are represented by the values of z-coordinates sampled on a grid of (x, y) values. Therefore, to create a surface plot we first need to generate a grid of (x, y) coordinates and find the height (z-coordinate) of the surface at each of the grid points. Note that you need to do the same thing for plotting a function of two variables. MATLAB provides a function meshgrid to create a grid of points over a specified range.

The function `meshgrid`: Suppose we want to plot a function $z = x^2 - y^2$ over the domain $0 \leq x \leq 4$ and $-4 \leq y \leq 4$. To do so, we first take several points in the domain, say 25 points, as shown in Fig. 5.6. We can create two matrices X and Y, each of size 5×5, and write the xy-coordinates of each point in these matrices. We can then evaluate z with the command `z = X.^2-Y.^2;`. Creating the two matrices X and Y is much easier with the `meshgrid` command:

```
rx = 0:4;              % create a vector rx=[0 1 2 3 4]
ry = -4:2:4;           % create a vector ry=[-4 -2 0 2 4]
[X,Y] = meshgrid(rx,ry); % create a grid of 25 points and
                       %- store their coordinates in X and Y.
```

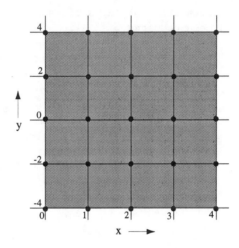

Figure 5.6: A grid of 25 points in the xy-plane. The grid can be created by the `meshgrid` command: `[X,Y] = meshgrid(rx,ry);` where rx and ry are vectors specifying the location of grid lines along x and y axes.

The commands shown above generate the 25 points shown in Fig. 5.6. All we need to generate is two vectors, `rx` and `ry`, to define the region of interest and distribution of grid points. Also, the two vectors need not be either same sized or linearly spaced (although most of the times we take square regions and create grid points equally spaced in both directions. See examples on pages 122–125). To be comfortable with 3-D graphics, you should understand the use of `meshgrid`.

Back to mesh plot: When a surface is plotted with `mesh(z)` (or `surf(z)`) command, where `z` is a matrix, then the tickmarks on the x and y axes do not indicate the domain of `z` but the row and column indices of the z-matrix. This is the default.

Typing `mesh(x,y,z)` or `surf(x,y,z)`, where x and y are vectors used by `meshgrid`
command to create a grid, results in the surface plot of z with x- and y-values shown
on the x and y axes. The following script file should serve as an example of how to
use `meshgrid` and `mesh` command. Here we try to plot the surface

$$z = \frac{xy(x^2 - y^2)}{x^2 + y^2}, \quad -3 \le x \le 3, \ -3 \le y \le 3$$

by computing the values of z over a 50×50 grid on the specified domain. The results
of the two plot commands are shown in Fig. 5.7.

```
%---------------------------------------------------------------------
% Script file to generate and plot the surface z =  xy(x^2-y^2)/(x^2+y^2)
% using meshgrid and mesh commands.
%---------------------------------------------------------------------
x=linspace(-3,3,50); y=x;        % Generate 50 element long vectors x and  y
[X,Y]=meshgrid(x,y);             % Create a grid over the specified domain
Z=X.*Y.*(X.^2-Y.^2)./(X.^2+Y.^2);
                                 % Calculate Z at each grid point (Z is 50X50)
mesh(x,y,Z)                      % Make a wire-frame surface plot of Z and
                                 %- use x and y values on the x and  y-axes.
figure(2)                        % Open a new figure window
meshc(x,y,Z),view(-55,20)        % Plot the same surface along with  contours
                                 %- and show the view from the specified angles.
```

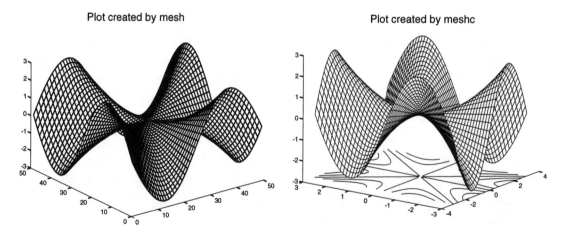

Figure 5.7: 3-D surface plots created by `mesh` and `meshc` commands. The second
plot uses a different viewing angle to show the center of the contour lines. Note that
the surfaces do not show hidden lines (this is the default setting; it can be changed
with the `hidden` command).

While surfaces created by `mesh` or its variants have a wire-frame appearance, surfaces created by the `surf` command or its variants produce a true surface-like appearance, especially when used with the `shading` command. There are three kinds of shading available— `shading flat` produces simple flat shading, `shading interp` produces more dramatic interpolated shading, and `shading faceted`, the default shading, shows shaded facets of the surface. Both `mesh` and `surf` can plot parametric surfaces with color scaling to indicate a fourth dimension. This is accomplished by giving four matrix arguments to these commands, e.g. `surf(X,Y,Z,C)` where X, Y, and Z are matrices representing a surface in parametric form and C is the matrix indicating color scaling. The command `surfl` can be used to control the light reflectance and to produce special effects with a specified location of a light source. See on line help on `surfl` for more information.

We close this section with a catalog of the popular 3D graphics functions. We hope that you can use these functions for your needs simply by following the example scripts. But we acknowledge that the `meshgrid` command takes some thought to understand well.

Function	Example Script	Output

plot3	Plot of a parametric space curve:
	
	$x(t) = t,\ y(t) = t^2,\ z(t) = t^3.$
	
	$0 \leq t \leq 1.$
	
	`t=linspace(0,1,100);`
	`x=t; y=t.^2; z=t.^3;`
	`plot3(x,y,z),grid`	

fill3	Plot of 4 filled polygons with 3 vertices each.
	
	`X=[0 0 0 0; 1 1 -1 1;`
	`    1 -1 -1 -1];`
	`Y=[0 0 0 0; 4 4 4 4;`
	`    4 4 4 4];`
	`Z=[0 0 0 0; 1 1 -1 -1;`
	`    -1 1 1 -1];`
	`fill3(X,Y,Z,rand(3,4))`
	`view(120,30)`	

contour3	Plot of 3-D contour lines of
	
	$z = -\dfrac{5}{1 + x^2 + y^2},$
	
	$\|x\| \leq 3, \|y\| \leq 3.$
	
	`r = linspace(-3,3,50);`
	`[x,y]=meshgrid(r,r);`
	`z=-5./(1+x.^2+y.^2);`
	`contour3(z)`	

Function	Example Script	Output
surf	$$z = \cos x \cos y \, e^{\frac{-\sqrt{x^2+y^2}}{4}}$$ $$|x| \leq 5, \quad |y| \leq 5$$ ```u = -.5:.2:.5; [X,Y] = meshgrid(u, u); Z = cos(X).*cos(Y).*... exp(-sqrt(X.^2+Y.^2)/4); surf(Z)```	
surfc	$$z = \cos x \cos y \, e^{\frac{-\sqrt{x^2+y^2}}{4}}$$ $$|x| \leq 5, \quad |y| \leq 5$$ ```u = -.5:.2:.5; [X,Y] = meshgrid(u, u); Z = cos(X).*cos(Y).*... exp(-sqrt(X.^2+Y.^2)/4); surfc(Z) view(-37.5,20) axis('off')```	
surfl	$$z = \cos x \cos y \, e^{\frac{-\sqrt{x^2+y^2}}{4}}$$ $$|x| \leq 5, \quad |y| \leq 5$$ ```u = -.5:.2:.5; [X,Y] = meshgrid(u, u); Z = cos(X).*cos(Y).*... exp(-sqrt(X.^2+Y.^2)/4); surfl(Z) shading interp colormap hot```	

Function	Example Script	Output

mesh	$$z = -\frac{5}{1+x^2+y^2}$$ $$|x| \le 3, \quad |y| \le 3$$ `x = linspace(-3,3,50);`
	`y = x;`
	`[x,y] = meshgrid(x,y);`
	`z=-5./(1+x.^2+y.^2);`
	`mesh(z)`	

meshz	$$z = -\frac{5}{1+x^2+y^2}$$ $$|x| \le 3, \quad |y| \le 3$$ `x = linspace(-3,3,50);`
	`y = x;`
	`[x,y] = meshgrid(x,y);`
	`z=-5./(1+x.^2+y.^2);`
	`meshz(z)`
	`view(-37.5, 50)`	

waterfall	$$z = -\frac{5}{1+x^2+y^2}$$ $$|x| \le 3, \quad |y| \le 3$$ `x = linspace(-3,3,50);`
	`y = x;`
	`[x,y] = meshgrid(x,y);`
	`z=-5./(1+x.^2+y.^2);`
	`waterfall(z)`	

Function	Example Script	Output
sphere	A unit sphere centered at the origin and generated by 3 matrices x, y, and z of size 21×21 each. ``` sphere(20) or [x,y,z]=sphere(20); surf(x,y,z) ```	

cylinder	A cylinder generated by
	
	$$r = \sin(3\pi z) + 2$$
	$$0 \le z \le 1, \quad 0 \le \theta \le 2\pi.$$
	
	``
	z=[0:.02:1]';
	r=sin(3*pi*z)+2;
	cylinder(r)
	``	

slice	Slices of the volumetric function
	
	$$f(x,y,z) = x^2 + y^2 - z^2$$
	$$\lvert x \rvert \le 3,\ \lvert y \rvert \le 3,\ \lvert z \rvert \le 3.$$
	
	``
	v = [-3:.2:3];
	[x,y,z]=meshgrid(v,v,v);
	f=(x.^2+y.^2-z.^2);
	xrows=[10,31]; yrows=28;
	zrows=16;
	slice(f,xrows,yrows,zrows,31);
	view([-30 30])
	``
	
	The value of the function is indicated by the color intensity.	

5.4 Handle Graphics

> You need not learn or understand Handle
> Graphics to do most of the plotting an ordi-
> nary person needs. If you want extra-detailed
> control of your graph appearance or want to
> do animation (beyond `comet` plots) you might
> want to learn Handle Graphics. This is NOT
> a topic for beginners.

A line is a graphics object. It has several properties—line style, color, thickness, visibility, etc. Once a line is drawn on the graphics screen, it is possible to change any of its properties later. Suppose you draw several lines with pencil on a paper. If you want to change one of the lines, you first must find the line you want to change and then change what you do not like about it. On the graphics screen, a line may be one among several graphics objects (e.g., axes, text, labels, etc.). So how do you get hold of a line? You get hold of a line by its *handle*.

What is a handle? MATLAB assigns a floating-point number to every object in the figure window (including invisible objects), and it uses this number as an address or name for the object in the figure. This number is the handle of the object.

Once you get hold of the handle, you can access all properties of the object. In short, the handle identifies the object and the object brings with it the list of its properties. In programming, this approach of defining objects and their properties is called *object-oriented programming*. The advantage it offers is that you can access individual objects and their properties and change any property of an object without affecting other properties or objects. Thus you get a complete control over graphics objects. MATLAB's entire system of object-oriented graphics and its user controllability is referred to as 'Handle Graphics™'. Here we briefly discuss this system and its usage, but we urge the more interested reader to consult the Users Guide [1] for more details.

The key to understanding and using Handle Graphics system is to know how to get the handles of graphics objects and how to use handles to get and change properties of the objects. Since not all graphics objects are independent (for example, the appearance of a line depends on the current axes in use), and a certain property of one may affect the properties of the others, it is also important to know how the objects are related.

5.4.1   The object hierarchy

Graphics objects follow a hierarchy of parent-child relationship. The following tree diagram shows the hierarchy.

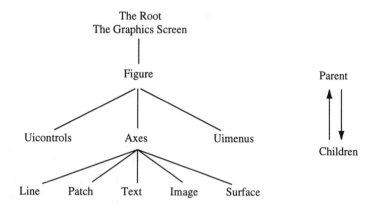

It is important to know this structure for two reasons:

- It shows you which objects will be affected if you change a default property value at a particular level, and

- It tells you at which level you can query for handles of which objects.

5.4.2   Object handles

Object handles are unique identifiers associated with each graphics object. These handles have a floating point representation. Handles are created at the time of creation of the object by graphics functions such as `plot(x,y)`, `contour(z)`, `line(z1,z2)`, and `text(xc,yc,'Look at this')`, etc.

Getting object handles

There are two ways of getting hold of handles:

1. By creating handles explicitly at the object-creation-level commands (that is, you can make a plot and get its handle at the same time):

```
hl = plot(x,y,'r-')     returns the handle of the line to hl.
hxl = xlabel('Angle')   returns the handle of the x-label to hxl.
```

2. By using explicit handle-returning functions:

gcf   gets the handle of the current figure.
                      Example: `hfig = gcf;` returns the handle of the current figure in `hfig`.

gca   gets the handle of the current axes.
                      Example: `haxes = gca;` returns the handle of the current axes in `haxes`.

gco   gets the handle of the current object.

Handles of other objects, in turn, can be obtained with the **get** command. For example, `hlines = get(gca,'children')` returns the handles of all *children* of the current axes in a column vector `hlines`. The function **get** is used to get a property value of an object, specified by its handle, in the command form

$$\boxed{\texttt{get}\,(handle,\,{}'PropertyName'\,).}$$

For an object with handle h, type `get(h)` to get a list of all property names and their current values.

Examples:

`hl = plot(x,y)`	plots a line and returns the handle `hl` of the plotted line.
`get(hl)`	lists all properties and property-values of the line.
`get(hl,'type')`	shows the type of the object (e.g. line, text, etc.)
`get(hl,'linestyle')`	returns the current line-style of the line.

For more information on **get**, see on-line help.

5.4.3 Object properties

Every graphics object on the screen has certain properties associated with it. For example, the properties of a line include type, parent, visible, color, linestyle, linewidth, xdata, ydata etc. Similarly, the properties of a text object, such as xlabel or title, include type, parent, visible, color, fontname, fontsize, fontweight, string, etc. Once the handle of an object is known, you can see the list of its properties and their current values with the command get(*handle*). For example, see Fig. 5.8 for the properties of a line and their current values.

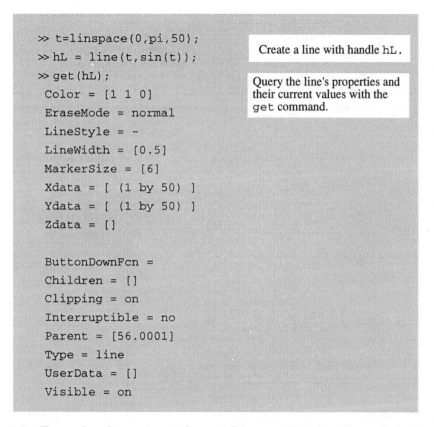

```
>> t=linspace(0,pi,50);          Create a line with handle hL.
>> hL = line(t,sin(t));
>> get(hL);                      Query the line's properties and
 Color = [1 1 0]                 their current values with the
 EraseMode = normal              get command.
 LineStyle = -
 LineWidth = [0.5]
 MarkerSize = [6]
 Xdata = [ (1 by 50) ]
 Ydata = [ (1 by 50) ]
 Zdata = []

 ButtonDownFcn =
 Children = []
 Clipping = on
 Interruptible = no
 Parent = [56.0001]
 Type = line
 UserData = []
 Visible = on
```

Figure 5.8: Example of creating a line with an explicit handle and finding the properties of the line along with their current values.

There are some properties common to all graphics objects. These properties are: children, clipping, parent, type, userdata, and visible.

Setting property values

You can see the list of properties and their values with the command set(*handle*).
Any property can be changed by the command

> set(*handle*, *'PropertyName'*, *PropertyValue'*)

where *PropertyValue* may be a character string or a number. If the *PropertyValue*
is a string then it must be enclosed within single quotes.

Fig. 5.9 shows the properties and property-values of a line.

```
>> t=linspace(0,pi,50);                    Create a line with handle hL.
>> x=t.*sin(t);
>> hL = line(t,x);                         Query the line's properties that
>> set(hL)                                 can be set and the available
                                           options.
 Color
 EraseMode: [ {normal} | background | xor | none ]
 LineStyle: [ {-} | -- | : | -. | + | o | * | . | x ]
 LineWidth
 MarkerSize
 Xdata
 Ydata
 Zdata

 ButtonDownFcn
 Clipping: [ {on} | off ]
 Interruptible: [ {no} | yes ]
 Parent
 UserData
 Visible: [ {on} | off ]
```

Figure 5.9: Example of creating a line with an explicit handle and finding the
properties of the line along with their possible values.

Now let us look at two examples:

Example-1: We create a line along with an explicit handle and then use the set
command to change the line style, its thickness, and some of the data. See
page 131.

Example-2: We write some text at a specified position (in the figure window),
create its handle, and then use the set command to change the fontsize, font,
and string of the text. See page 132.

Example Script	Output

Create a simple line plot and assign its handle to hL.

```
t=linspace(0,pi,50);
x=t.*sin(t);
hL = line(t,x);
```

Change the line style to dashed.

```
set(hL,'linestyle','--')
```

Change the line thickness.

```
set(hL,'linewidth','3')
```

Change the values of some y-coordinates.

```
yvec=get(hL,'ydata');
yvec(25:35)=ones(size(yvec(25:35)));
set(hL,'ydata',yvec)
```

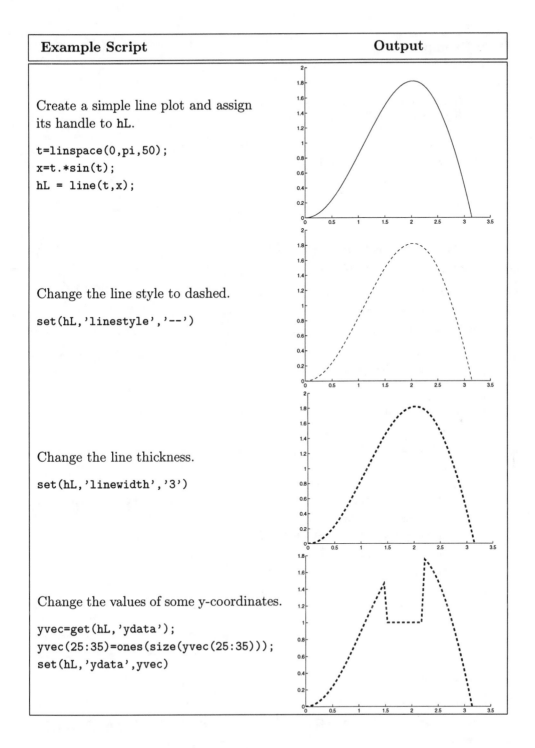

Example Script	Output

Write some text at the location (0.5,0.5)
and create a handle for it.

```
x=0.5; y=0.5;
hT = text(x,y,'This is Cool',...
    'erasemode','xor')
```

Make the text centered at (0.5,0.5) and
change the font and fontsize.

```
set(hT, 'horizontal','center','fontsize',36,...
    'fontname','symbol')
set(gca,'visible','off')
```

Now, create a template for presentation.

```
clg
line([0 0 1 1 0],[0 1 1 0 0]);
h1=text(.5,.7,'Coming Soon...',...
    'fontangle','italic',...
    'horizontal','center');
set(gca,'visible','off')
h2=text(.5,.5,'3D-Simulation',...
    'horizontal','center',...
    'fontsize',40,'fontname','times',...
    'fontweight','bold','erase','xor');
h3=text(.5,.4,'by','horizontal','center');
h4=text(.5,.3,'Stephen Spielberg',...
    'fontsize',16,'horizontal','center',...
    'erase','xor');
```

Next slide please...

```
set(h1,'string','')
set(h2,'string','The Model')
set(h3,'string','')
set(h4,'string','Assumptions & Idealizations')
```

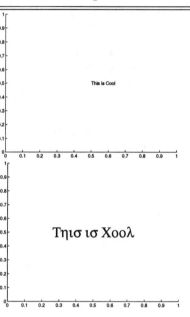

5.4.4 Modifying an existing plot

Even if you create a plot without explicitly creating object handles, MATLAB creates handles for each object on the plot. If you want to modify any object, you have to first get its handle. Here is where you need to know the parent-child relationship among several graphics objects. The following example illustrates how to get the handle of different objects and use the handles to modify the plot.

We take Fig. 5.1 on page 106 and use the aforementioned Handle Graphics features to modify the figure. The following script file is used to change the plot in Fig. 5.1 to the one shown in Fig. 5.10. You may find the following script file confusing because it uses a vector of handles, `hline`, and accesses different elements of this vector, without much explanation. Hopefully, your confusion will be cleared after you read the next section *Understanding a vector of handles*.

```
h=gca;                              % get the handle of the current axes
set(h,'box','off');                 % throw away the enclosing box frame
hline=get(h,'children');            % get the handles of children of axes
                                    %%% Note that hline is a vector of
                                    %%% handles because h has many  children
set(hline(7),'linewidth',4)         % change the line width of the 1st  line
set(hline(6),'visible','off')       % make the 'lin. approx' line  invisible
delete(hline(3))                    % delete the text 'linear  approximation'
hxl=get(h,'xlabel');                % get the handle of xlabel
set(hxl,'string','t (angle)')       % change the text of xlabel
set(hxl,'fontname','times')         % change the font of xlabel
set(hxl,'fontsize',20,'fontweight','bold')
                                    % change the font-size & font-weight
```

Understanding a vector of handles: In the above script file you may perhaps be confused about the use of the handle `hline`. The command, `hline = get(h,'children')`, above gets the handles of all the children of the current axes (specified by handle h) in a column vector `hline`. The vector `hline` has seven elements—three handles for the three lines and four handles for the four text objects (created by `text` and `gtext` commands). So, how do we know which handle is for which line or text? The command `get(hline($i$),'type')` lists the type of the object whose handle is `hline($i$)`. The confusion is not clear yet. What if `hline(5)`, `hline(6)`, and `hline(7)` are all lines? How do we know which handle corresponds to which line? Once we know the type of the object, we can identify its handle, among several similar object handles, by querying a more distinctive property of

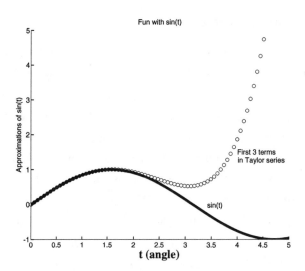

Figure 5.10: Example of manipulation of a figure with Handle Graphics. This figure is a result of executing the above script file after generating Fig. 5.1

the object, such as **linestyle** for lines and **string** for text objects. For example, consider the handle vector **hline** above. Then,

get(hline(5),'linestyle')   returns 'o ' for the linestyle,

get(hline(6),'linestyle')   returns '--' for the linestyle,

get(hline(1),'string')   returns 'in Taylor series' for the string, and

get(hline(2),'string')   returns 'First 3 terms' for the string.

From this example, it should be clear that *the handles of children of the axes are listed in the stacking order of the objects*, i.e., the last object added goes on the top of the stack. Thus the elements of the handle vector correspond to the objects in the reverse order of their creation!

5.4.5   Deleting graphics objects

Any object in the graphics window can be deleted without disturbing the other objects with the command

delete(ObjHandle)

where *ObjHandle* is the handle of the object. We have used this command in the script file which produced Fig. 5.10 to delete the text 'linear approximation' from the figure. We could have used **delete(hline(6))** to delete the corresponding line rather than making it invisible.

5.4.6 A complete control over graphics layout

We close this section with an example of arbitrary placement of axes and figures in the graphics window. With Handle Graphics tools like these you have almost complete control of the graphics layout. Here is a simple example. The output appears in Fig. 5.11

```
%-----------------------------------------------------------------
%       Example of graphics placement with Handle Graphics
%-----------------------------------------------------------------
clf                                % clear all previous figures
t=linspace(0,2*pi);
y=sin(t);
%--------------------
h1=axes('position',[0.1 0.1 .8 .8]);  % place axes with width .8 and  height
                                   %- .8 at coordinates (.1,.1)
plot(t,y),xlabel('t'),ylabel('sin t')
set(h1,'Box','Off');               % Turn the enclosing box off
xhl=get(gca,'xlabel');             % get the handle of 'xlabel' of the
                                   %- current axes and assign to  xlh
set(xhl,'fontsize',16,'fontweight','bold')
                                   % change attributes of 'xlabel'
yhl=get(gca,'ylabel');             % do the same with 'ylabel'
set(yhl,'fontsize',16,'fontweight','bold')
%--------------------

h2=axes('position',[0.6 0.6 .2 .2]);  % place another axes on the  same plot
fill(t,y.^2,'r')                   % draw a filled polygon with
red fill
set(h2,'Box','Off');
xlabel('t'),ylabel('(sin t)^2')
set(get(h2,'XLabel'),'FontName','Times')
set(get(h2,'yLabel'),'FontName','Times')

%--------------------
h3=axes('position',[0.15 0.2 .3 .3]); % place yet another axes
polar(t,y./t);                     % make a polar plot
polarch=get(gca,'children');       % get the handle of all the  children
                                   %- of the current axes
set(polarch(1),'linewidth',3)      % set the line width of the  first child
                                   %- which is actually the line  we plotted
for i=1:length(polarch)            % let us clear the clutter due  to text
    if strcmp(get(polarch(i),'type'),'text')
                                   % look for all 'text'  children
        delete(polarch(i))         % delete all text children
    end end
%--------------------
```

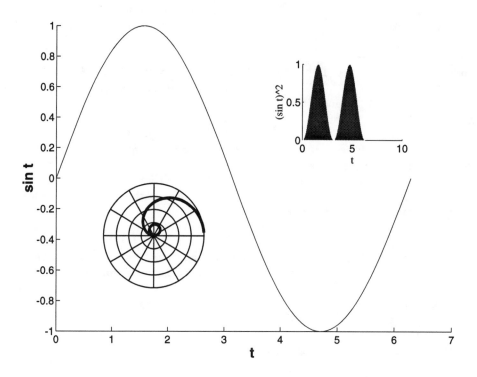

Figure 5.11: Example of manipulation of the Figure Window with Handle Graphics. Virtually anything in the figure window, including the placement of axes, can be manipulated with Handle Graphics.

5.5 Saving and Printing Graphs

The simplest way to get a hardcopy of a graph is to type `print` in the command window after the graph appears in the figure window. The `print` command sends the graph in the current figure window to the default printer in an appropriate form. On PCs (running Windows) and Macs you could, alternatively, activate the figure window (bring to the front by clicking on it) and then select `print` from the file menu.

The figure can also be saved into a specified file in the PostScript or Encapsulated PostScript (EPS) format. These formats are available for black and white as well as color printers. The PostScript supported includes both Level 1 and Level 2 PostScript. The command to save graphics to a file has the form

$$\boxed{\texttt{print -d}\textit{devicetype} \texttt{ -}\textit{options} \textit{ filename}}$$

where *devicetype* for PostScript printers can be one of the following:

devicetype	Description	devicetype	Description
ps	black and white PostScript	eps	black and white EPSF
psc	color PostScript	epsc	color EPSF
ps2	Level2 BW PostScript	eps2	Level 2 black and white EPSF
psc2	Level 2 color PostScript	epsc	Level 2 color EPSF.

For example, the command

$$\texttt{print -deps sineplot}$$

saves the current figure in the Encapsulated PostScript file `sineplot.eps`. The '.eps' extension is automatically generated by MATLAB .

The standard optional argument *-options* supported are `append`, `epsi`, `Pprinter`, and `fhandle`. There are several other platform dependent options. See on-line help on `print` for more information.

In addition to the PostScript devices, MATLAB supports a number of other printer devices on UNIX and PC systems. There are device options available for HP Laser Jet, Desk Jet, and Paint Jet printers, DEC LN03 printer, Epson printers and other types of printers. See on-line help on `print` to check the available devices and options.

Other than printer devices, MATLAB can also generate a graphics file in the Adobe Illustrator format by specifying `-dill` in the `-d`*devicetype* field of the `print` command. This option is quite useful if you want to dress-up or modify the figure in a way that is extremely difficult to do in MATLAB. Of course, you must have access to Adobe Illustrator to be able to open and edit the saved graphs. Figure 5.12 shows an example of a graph generated in MATLAB and then modified in Adobe Illustrator. The most annoying aspect of MATLAB 4.x's graphics is the lack of simple facilities to write subscripts and superscripts and mix fonts in the labels. There is no way of producing something like $\sin(\lambda^2_{\text{critical}})$ as the label on the axes without playing with the PostScript file (MathWorks says it will incorporate such features in future versions of mat)!

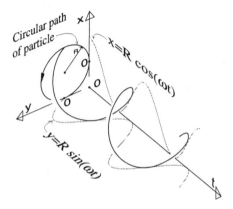

Figure 5.12: Example of a figure generated in MATLAB, saved in the Illustrator format and then modified in Adobe Illustrator. The rotation and shearing of texts was done in Illustrator (courtesy A. Ruina).

The background color of the hardcopy

The figures in MATLAB appear on a black background on the screen. When the figures are saved in a file or printed on paper, the colors are reversed. If you wish to make a hardcopy with black background and lines drawn in white, type the command

```
set(gcf,'inverthardcopy', 'off')
```

before sending the print command. A number of figures in this book were made this way.

5.6 Animation

We all know the visual impact of animation. If you have a lot of data representing
a function or a system at several time sequences, you may wish to take advantage
of MATLAB's capability to animate your data.

There are three types of facilities for animation in MATLAB.

1. **Comet plot:** This is the simplest and the most restricted facility to display a
   2-D or 3-D line graph as an animated plot. The command comet(x,y) plots
   the data in vectors x and y with a comet moving through the data points.
   The trail of the comet traces a line connecting the data points. So, rather
   than having the entire plot appear on the screen at once, you can see the
   graph 'being plotted'. This facility may be useful in visualizing trajectories in
   a phase plane. For an example, see the built-in demo on the Lorenz attractor.

2. **Movies:** If you have a sequence of plots that you would like to animate, use
   the built-in movie facility. The basic idea is to store each figure as a frame
   of the movie, with each frame stored as a column vector of a big matrix, say
   M, and then to play the frames on the screen with the command movie(M). A
   frame is stored in a column vector using the command getframe. For efficient
   storage you should first initialize the matrix M. The built-in command moviein
   is provided precisely for this initialization, although you can do it yourself too.
   An example script file to make a movie might look like this:

```
%---- skeleton of a script file to generate and play a movie  ------
%
nframes = 36;                % number of frames in the the movie
Frames = moviein(nframes);   % initialize the matrix 'Frames'
for i = 1:nframes
   :                         % you may have calculations here to
   :                         %- generate data
   :
   x = ....;
   y = ....;
   plot(x,y)                 % you may use any plotting function
   Frames(:,i) = getframe;   % store the current figure as a  frame
end
movie(Frames,5)              % play the movie stored in frames 5 times
```

You can also specify the speed (frames/second) at which you want to play the movie (the actual speed will eventually depend on your CPU) by typing `movie(Frames,`*m, fps*`)`, which plays the movie, stored in `Frames`, *m* times at the rate *fps* frames per second.

3. **Handle Graphics:** Another way, and perhaps the most versatile way, of creating animation is to use the Handle Graphics facilities. The basic idea here is to plot an object on the screen, get its handle, use the handle to change the desired properties of the object (most likely its 'xdata' and 'ydata' values), and replot the object over a selected sequence of times. There are two important things to know to be able to create animation using Handle Graphics:

   - The command `drawnow`, which flushes the graphics output to the screen without waiting for the control to return to MATLAB. The on-line help on `drawnow` explains how it works.

   - The object property 'erasemode' which can be set to 'normal', 'background', 'none', or 'xor' to control the appearance of the object when the graphics screen is redrawn. For example, if a script file containing the following lines is executed

```
h1 = plot(x1,y1,'erasemode','none');
h2 = plot(x2,y2,'erasemode','xor');
:
newx1=...; newy1=...; newx2=...; newy2=...;
:
set(h1,'xdata',newx1,'ydata',newy1);
set(h2,'xdata',newx2,'ydata',newy2);
:
```

   then the first `set` command draws the first object with the new x-data and y-data, but the same object drawn before remains on the screen, while the second `set` command redraws the second object with new data and also erases the object drawn with the previous data x2 and y2. Thus it is possible to keep some objects fixed on the screen while some other objects change with each pass of a control flow.

Now, let us look at some examples.

Example-1: A bead goes around a circular path: The basic idea is to first
calculate various positions of the bead along the circular path, draw the bead as a
point at the initial position and create its handle, and then use the handle to set
the x- and y-coordinates of the bead to new values inside a loop that cycles through
all positions. The `erasemode` property of the bead is set to `xor` (Exclusive Or) so
that the old bead is erased from the screen when the new bead is drawn. Try the
following script file.

```
% Script file for animating the circular motion of a bead
% ---------------------------------------------
clg                              % clear any previous graph
theta=linspace(0,2*pi,100);      % create a vector theta
x=cos(theta);                    % generate x and y-coordinates
y=sin(theta);                    %- of the bead along the path
hbead=line(x(1),y(1),'linestyle','o','markersize',8,'erase','xor');
                                 % draw the bead at the initial
                                 %- position and assign a handle
axis([-1 1 -1 1]); axis('square');
for k=2:length(theta)            % cycle through all positions
    set(hbead,'xdata',x(k),'ydata',y(k));
                                 % draw the bead at the new position
    drawnow
end
```

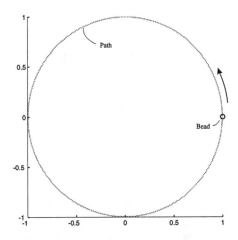

Figure 5.13: A bead goes on a circular path.

Example-2: The bead going around a circular path leaves its trail: In
Example-1 above, the bead goes on the circular path, but it does not clearly seem
that it traverses a circle. To make it clear, we can make the bead leave a trail as
it moves. For this purpose, we basically draw the bead twice, once as a bead (with
bigger marker size) and once as a point at each location. But we set the `erasemode`
property of the point to `none` so that the point (the previous position of the bead)
remains on the screen as the bead moves and thus creates a trail of the bead.

```
% Script file for animating the circular motion of a bead. As the
% bead moves, it leaves a trail behind it.
% ---------------------------------------------
clg
theta=linspace(0,2*pi,100);
x=cos(theta); y=sin(theta);
hbead=line(x(1),y(1),'linestyle','o','markersize',8,'erase','xor');
htrail=line(x(1),y(1),'linestyle','.','erase','none');
axis([-1 1 -1 1]);
axis('square');
for k=2:length(theta)
    set(hbead,'xdata',x(k),'ydata',y(k));
    set(htrail,'xdata',x(k),'ydata',y(k));
    drawnow end
```

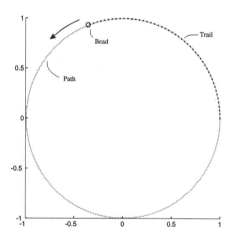

Figure 5.14: A bead goes on a circular path and leaves a trail behind it.

Example-3: A bar pendulum swings in 2D: Here is a slightly more complicated example. It involves animation of the motion of a bar pendulum governed
by the ODE $\ddot{\theta} + \sin\theta = 0$. Now that you are comfortable with defining graphics
objects and using their handles to change their position etc., the added complication
of solving a differential equation shouldn't be too hard.

```
%----- script file to animate a bar pendulum --------------

   clf                       % clear figure and stuff
   data=[0 0; -1.5 0];       % coordinates of endpoints of the bar
   phi=0;                    % initial orientation
   R=[cos(phi) -sin(phi); +sin(phi) cos(phi)];
                             % rotation matrix
   data=R*data;
   axis([-2 2 -2 2])         % set axis limits
   axis('equal')

   %-----define the objects called bar, hinge, and path.
   bar=line('xdata',data(1,:),'ydata',data(2,:),'linewidth',3,'erase','xor') ;
   hinge=line('xdata',0,'ydata',0,'linestyle','o','markersize',[10]);
   path=line('xdata',[],'ydata', [],'linestyle','.','erasemode','none');

   theta=pi-pi/1000;         % initial angle
   thetadot=0;               % initial angular speed
   dt=.2; tfinal=50; t=0;    % time step, initial and final time

   %------Euler's method for numerical integration
   while(t<tfinal);
       t=t+dt;
       theta=theta + thetadot*dt;
       thetadot=thetadot -sin(theta)*dt;
       R=[cos(theta) (-sin(theta)); sin(theta) cos(theta)];
       datanew= R*data;

       %---- change the property values of the objects: path and bar.
       set(path,'xdata', datanew(1,1), 'ydata', datanew(2,1) );
       set(bar,'xdata',datanew(1,:),'ydata',datanew(2,:) );
       drawnow;
   end
```

Example-4: The bar pendulum swings, and other data are displayed:
Now here is the challenge. If you can understand the following script file, you
are in good shape! You are ready to do almost any animation. The following
example divides the graphics screen in four parts, shows the motion of the pendulum
in one part, shows the position of the tip in the second part, plots the angular
displacement θ in the third part and the angular speed $\dot{\theta}$ in the fourth part (see
Fig. 5.15). There are four animations occurring simultaneously. Try it! There is
an intentional bug in one of the four animations. If you start the pendulum from
the vertical upright position with an initial angular speed (you will need to change
`thetadot = 0` statement inside the program for this) then you should see the bug.
Go ahead, find the bug and fix it.

```
%----- script file to animate a bar pendulum with animated data  ----------
%%% get basic data for animation
% ask the user for initial position
disp('Please specify the initial angle from the')
disp('vertical upright position.'), disp(' ')
offset = input('Enter the initial angle now (e.g. pi/100): ');

% ask the user for time of simulation
tfinal = input('Please enter the duration of simulation (e.g. 50): ');
disp('I am working....')

tf = tfinal;
theta=pi-offset;        % initial angle
thetadot=0;             % initial angular speed
dt=.2; t=0;  tf=tf;     % time step, initial and final time

clf                     % clear figure and stuff
h1=axes('position',[0.6 .5 .4 .3]);
axis([0 tf -4 4]);      % set axis limits
xlabel('time'), ylabel('displacement')
Displ=line('xdata',[],'ydata',
[],'linestyle','.','erasemode','none');

h2=axes('position',[0.6 .1 .4 .3]);
axis([0 tf -4 4]);      % set axis limits
xlabel('time'),ylabel('velocity')
Vel=line('xdata',[],'ydata',[],'linestyle','.','erasemode','none');

h3=axes('position',[.1 .0 .4 .4]);
axis([-2 2 -2 2])       % set axis limits
axis('equal') axis('off')
tip=line('xdata',[],'ydata', [],'linestyle','o',...
        'markersize',8,'erasemode','xor');
```

```
h4=axes('position',[.1 .4 .4 .4]);
axis([-2 2 -2 2])          % set axis limits
axis('equal')


data=[0 0; -1.8 0];        % coordinates of endpoints of the bar
phi=0;                     % initial orientation
R=[cos(phi) -sin(phi); +sin(phi) cos(phi)];
                           % rotation matrix data=R*data;


%-----define the objects called bar, hinge, and path.
bar=line('xdata',data(1,:),'ydata',data(2,:),'linewidth',3,'erase','xor') ;
hinge=line('xdata',0,'ydata',0,'linestyle','o','markersize',[10]);
path=line('xdata',[],'ydata', [],'linestyle','.','erasemode','none');


%------Euler's method for numerical integration
while(t<tfinal);
   t=t+dt;
   theta=theta + thetadot*dt;
   thetadot=thetadot -sin(theta)*dt;
   R=[cos(theta) (-sin(theta)); sin(theta) cos(theta)];
   datanew= R*data;

   axes(h3);
   %---- change the property values of the objects: path and bar.
   set(path,'xdata', datanew(1,1), 'ydata', datanew(2,1) );
   set(bar,'xdata',datanew(1,:),'ydata',datanew(2,:) );
   axes(h3);
   set(tip,'xdata', datanew(1,1), 'ydata', 0);
   axes(h1);
   set(Displ,'xdata', t, 'ydata', theta );
   axes(h2);
   set(Vel,'xdata', t, 'ydata', thetadot );
   drawnow;
end
```

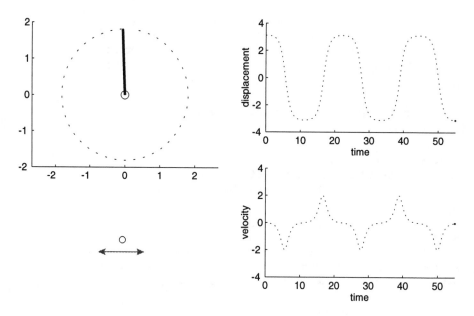

Figure 5.15: Animation of motion of a bar pendulum along with animation of position and velocity data.

6. *Errors*

Errors are an integral part of life whether you interact with computers or not. The only difference is, when you interact with computers your errors are pointed out immediately—often bluntly and without much advice. Interaction with MATLAB is no exception. Yes, to err is human, but to forgive is definitely not MATLABine. So, the earlier you get used to the blunt manners of your friend and his terse comments, the better for you. Since this friend does not offer much advice most of the time, we give you some hints here based on our own experience of dealing with your friend. Before we begin, we warn you that this friend has a tendency of becoming very irritating if you work under too much time pressure or don't have enough sleep. In particular, if you are not relaxed enough to distinguish between '(' and '[', ';' and ':', or 'a' and 'A', you and your friend are going to have long sessions staring at each other.

Here are the most common error messages, in alphabetical order (according to the first word that is not an article or a preposition), that you are likely to get while working in MATLAB. All messages below are shown following a typical command. Following the actual message are explanations and tips.

- ```
  >> D(2:3,:)=sin(d)
  ???  In an assignment A(matrix,:) = B, the number
  of columns in A and B must be the same.
  ```

  This is typical problem in matrix assignments where the dimensions of the matrices on the two sides of the equal sign do not match. Use the `size` and `length` commands to check the dimensions on both sides and make sure they agree.

147
  ```

For example, for the above command to execute properly, `size(D(2:3,:)` and `size(sin(d))` or `size(d)` must give the same dimensions.

A similar error occurs when trying to assign a matrix to a vector:

```
      >> D(:,2)=d1
???  In an assignment  A(matrix) = B, a vector A
can't be resized to a matrix.
```

In this example, D and d1 are matrices, but `D(:,2)` is a vector (the second column of D), so d1 cannot fit into `D(:,2)`.

- ```
  >> (x,y)=circlefn(5);
  ???  (x,
  
       |
  
  A closing right parenthesis is missing.
  Check for a missing ")" or a missing operator.
  ```

  Here, neither a right parenthesis nor an operator is missing, but MATLAB is confused with the list of variables because a list within *parenthesis* represents matrix indices. When the variables represent output of a function or a list of vectors, they must be enclosed within *square brackets*. The correct command here is `[x,y]=circlefn(5)` (`circlefn` is a user-written function). When parentheses and brackets are mixed up, the same error message is displayed:

  ```
  (x,y]=circlefn(5);
  ???  (x,
  
       |
  
  A closing right parenthesis is missing.
  Check for a missing ")" or a missing operator.
  ```

- ```
  x=1:10;
  v=[0 3 6];
  x(v)
  ???  Index into matrix is negative or zero.
  ```

  The first element of the index vector v is zero. Thus we are trying to get the zeroth element of x. But zero is not a valid index for any matrix or vector in MATLAB. The same problem arises when a negative number appears as an index. Also, of course, an error occurs when the specified index exceeds the corresponding dimension of the variable:

  ```
  x(12)
  ???  Index exceeds matrix dimensions.
  ```

The examples given here for index-dimension mismatch are almost trivial. Most of the times these problems arise when matrix indices are created, incremented, and manipulated inside loops.

- ```
  >> x=1:10; y=10:-2:-8;
  >> x*y
  ??? Error using ==> *
  Inner matrix dimensions must agree.
  ```

In matrix multiplication x*y the number of rows of x must equal the number of columns of y. Here x and y are both row vectors of size 1×10 and therefore, cannot multiply. However, x*y' and x'*y will both execute without error, producing inner and outer products respectively.

Several other operations involving matrices of improper dimensions produce similar errors. A general rule is to write the expression on paper and think if the operation makes mathematical sense. If not, then MATLAB is likely to give you error. For example, A^2 makes sense for a matrix A only if the matrix is square, and A^x for a vector x and matrix A does not make any sense. The exceptions to this rule are the two division operators—'/' and '\'. While y/x, for the two vectors defined above, may not make any sense mathematically, MATLAB gives an answer:

```
>> y/x
ans =
   -0.2857
```

This is because this division is not just division in MATLAB, but it also gives solutions to matrix equations. For rectangular matrices it gives solutions in the least squares sense. See on-line help on slash for more details.

A common source of error is to use the matrix operators where you want array operators. For example, for the vectors x and y above, y.^x gives element-by-element exponentiation, but y^x produces an error:

```
>> y^x
??? Error using ==> ^
Matrix dimensions must agree.
```

- ```
  [x,y]=Circlefn;
  ??? Input argument r is undefined.

  Error in ==> Macintosh HD:MATLAB 4.1:Circlefn.m
  ```

```
On line 4  ==> x = r*cos(theta); y = ....
```

A function file has been executed without giving proper input. This is one of the very few error messages that provides enough information (the function name, the name of the directory where the function file is located, and the line number where the error occurred).

- ```
  >> [t,x]=Circle(5);
  ??? [t,x]=Circle
               |
  M-file scripts return no outputs.
  ```

Here Circle is a script file. Input-output lists cannot be specified with script files. But here is a slightly more interesting case that produces the same error. The error occurs in trying to execute the following function file:

```
Function [x,y] = circlefn(r);
% CIRCLEFN - Function to draw a circle of radius r.
theta = linspace(0,2*pi,100);      % create vector theta
x = r*cos(theta); y = r*cos(theta); % generate coordinates
plot(x,y);                         % plot the circle
```

Here is the error:

```
>> [x,y]=circlefn(5)
??? [x,y]=circlefn
               |
M-file scripts return no outputs.
```

You scream, "Hey, it's not a script!" True, but it's not a function either. For it to qualify as a function, the f in function, in the definition line, must also be in lower case which is not the case here. So MATLAB gets confused. Yes, the error message could have been better, but you are probably going to say this in quite a few cases.

- ```
  [x,y]=Circlefn();
  ??? [x,y]=Circlefn()
                    |
  Missing variable or function.
  ```

This is an obvious one—the input variable is missing. MATLAB expects to see a variable or a function name within the parentheses.

- CIRCLEFN[5];
  ??? CIRCLEFN[

          |

  Missing operator, comma, or semi-colon.

  Here parentheses are required in the place of the square brackets. The error locator bar is at the right place and should help. But what is missing is neither an *operator* nor a *comma* nor a *semi-colon*. This error message is perhaps the most frequent one and also the most useless one in terms of helping you out. See the appearance of this message in various cases below.

  Circle(5);
  ??? Circle(

       |

  Missing operator, comma, or semi-colon.

  Circle is a script file and cannot take an input as an argument. Again, the error message does not help much.

  EIG(D)
  ??? EIG(

      |

  Missing operator, comma, or semi-colon.

  Here EIG is a built-in function and its name must be typed in lower case: eig. MATLAB does not recognize EIG, and hence the error.

- >> x = b+2.33
  ??? Undefined function or variable b.

  The variable b has not been defined. This message is right on target. But when the same message comes for a function or script which you have written, you may scratch your head. In such cases, the function or the script that you are trying to execute is most probably in a different directory than the current directory. Use what, dir, or ls to show the list of files in the current directory. If the file is not listed there then MATLAB cannot access it. You may have to locate the directory of the file with the command which *filename* and then change the working directory with the cd command to the desired directory.

- plot(d,d1)
  ??? Error using ==> plot
  Vectors must be the same lengths.

The input vectors in `plot` command must be pair-wise compatible. For a detailed discussion of this, see the description of the plot command in Section 5.

7. *What Else is There?*

7.1 The Symbolic Math Toolbox

The *Basic* MATLAB does not do symbolic mathematics. There are, however, two toolboxes (optional packages) available for this purpose— the Symbolic Math Toolbox and the Extended Symbolic Math Toolbox. The first one provides facilities for interactive computer algebra, the second one extends the facility to programming and adds more algebraic functions. The *student edition* of MATLAB comes with the Symbolic Math Toolbox.

The Symbolic Math Toolboxes of MATLAB are built on Maple, a computer algebra system. When you do symbolic mathematics, MATLAB acts as a messenger between you and Maple—it takes your commands to Maple, Maple executes your commands and hands over the results to MATLAB , and MATLAB brings the results to you. You perhaps know what happens when a middleman is involved—it is often more counterproductive. That is precisely our experience with MATLAB's Symbolic Math Toolbox. There is more clutter because you not only have to know the Maple commands but also the the MATLAB interface for them. Moreover, the way you enter commands depends on context. Our recommendation—work in Maple directly. If you are a student, the student edition of Maple is cheap enough. If you want the full functionality of Maple, the Extended Math Toolbox of MATLAB is definitely *not* the way to go. You lose most of Maple's graphics capability.

MATLAB's Symbolic Toolbox is ok if you do not have to pay extra for it (i.e., the Student Edition) and if you need to do just a little bit of symbolic computation now and then. If you use Mathematica or Macsyma, you are in good shape, too. Both packages provide M-file support for MATLAB.

There are mainly three other significant facilities in MATLAB, which we do not in depth discuss here.

7.2   Debugging Tools

The new versions of MATLAB (version 4.x) support a built-in debugger which consists of 10 commands — dbclear, dbcont, dbdown, dbquit, dbstack, dbstatus, dbstep, dbstop, dbtype, and dbup, to help you debug your MATLAB programs. See the on-line help under lang for details of these commands.

7.3   External Interface: Mex-files

If you wish to dynamically link your Fortran or C programs to MATLAB functions so that they can communicate and exchange data, you need to learn about *MEX*-files. Consult the External Interface Guide [3] to learn about these files. The process of developing Mex-files is fairly complicated and highly system-dependent. You should perhaps first consider non-dynamic linking with your external programs through standard ASCII data files.

7.4   Graphics User Interface

It is also possible to design your own Graphical User Interface (GUI) with menus, buttons, and slider controls in MATLAB. This facility is very useful if you are developing an application package to be used by others. You can build many visual 'user-friendly' features in your application. For more information consult MATLAB's Building a Graphical User Interface Guide [4].

A. The MATLAB Language Reference

A.1 Punctuation Marks and Other Symbols

On-line help topic: `punct`

,   **Comma:** A comma is used to:

- separate variables in the input and output list of a function,
  Example: `[t,x]=ode23('pend',t0,tf,x0)`,
- separate the row and column indices in a matrix,
  Example: `A(m,n)`, `A(1:10,3)` etc.,
- separate different commands on the same line.
  Example: `plot(x,y)`, `grid`, `xlabel('x')` etc.

;   **Semicolon:** A semicolon is used to:

- suppress the MATLAB output of a command,
  Example: `x=1:10; y=A*x;` etc.,
- separate rows in the input list of a matrix.
  Example: `A=[1 2; 4 9]`.

:   **Colon:** A colon is used to specify range:

- in creating vectors,
  Example: `x=1:10; y=1:2:100;` etc.
- for matrix and vector indices,
  Example: see Section 3.1.3,
- in `for` loops.
  Example: `for i=1:20, x=x+i; end`.

'   **Right Quote:** A single right quote is used to transpose a vector or a matrix.

       Example: `symA = (A'+A)/2.`

' '   **Single Quotes:** A pair of single right quote characters is used to enclose a character string.

       Example: `xlabel('time'), title('My plot')` etc.

.   **Period:** A period is used:

- as a decimal point,
- in array operations.

       Example: `Asq = A.^2` (see page 3.2.1).

..   **Two periods:** Two periods are used in `cd ..` command to access parent directory

...   **Ellipsis:** Ellipsis (three periods) at the end of a command denote continuation to the next line.

       Example: `x = [log(1:100) sin(v+a.*b) 22.3 23.0 34.0 ...`
          `33.0 40:50 80];`

!   **Exclamation:** An exclamation preceding a *command* is used to send the local operating system command *command* to the system. This command is not applicable to Macs.

       Example: `!emacs newfile.m` invokes the local emacs editor.

%   **Percent:** A percent character is used to:

- used to mark the beginning of a comment, except when used in character strings,

       Example: `% This is a comment,` but `rate = '8.5%'` is a string,

- to denote formats in standard I/O functions `sprintf` and `fprintf`.

       Example: `sprintf('R = %6.4f', r).`

( )   **Parentheses:** Parentheses are used to:

- specify precedence in arithmetic operations,

       Example: `a = 5/(2+x*(3-i));` etc.,

- enclose matrix and vector indices,

       Example: `A(1:5,2) = 5; v = x(1:n-5);` etc.,

- enclose the list of input variables of a function.

       Example: `[t,x]=ode23('pend', t0, tf, x0).`

[ ]   **Square brackets:** Square brackets are used to:

- form and concatenate vectors and matrices,

       Example: `v = [1 2 3:9]; X = [v; log(v)];` etc.,

- enclose the list of output variables of a function.

       Example: `[V,D] = eig(A);` etc.

A.2 General-Purpose Commands

See Section 1.6.6

On-line help category: `general`

Help & Query			
`lookfor`	Keyword search for help	`whatsnew`	Display ReadMe files
`help`	On-line help	`what`	List files in the directory
`demo`	Run demo program	`which`	Locate a file
`info`	Info about MATLAB	`why`	Give philosophic advice
`ver`	MATLAB version info	`path`	List accessible directories

Command Window Control			
`clc`	Clear command window	`home`	Send cursor home
`format`	Set screen output format	`echo`	Echo commands in script file
`more`	Control paged screen output	`↑, ↓`	Recall previous commands

Working with Files & Directories			
`pwd`	Show current directory	`delete`	Delete file
`cd`	Change current directory	`diary`	Save text of MATLAB session
`dir, ls`	List directory contents	`type`	Show contents of file
`!`	Access operating system	`unix`	Execute Unix command

Variable and Workspace			
`clear`	Clear variables and functions	`length`	Length of a vector
`who,whos`	List current variables	`size`	Size of a matrix
`load`	Load variables from file	`pack`	Consolidate memory space
`save`	Save variables in MAT-file	`disp`	Display text or matrix

Start & Exit			
`matlabrc`	Master startup file	`quit`	Quit MATLAB
`startup`	M-file executed at startup	`exit`	Same as quit

Time & Date			
`clock`	Wall clock time	`etime`	Elapsed time function
`cputime`	Elapsed CPU time	`tic`	Start stopwatch timer
`date`	Date, month, year	`toc`	Read stopwatch timer

A.3   Special Variables and Constants

Constants		Variables	
`pi`	π (=3.14159...)	`ans`	Default output variable
`inf`	∞ (infinity)	`flops`	Count of floating point operations
`NaN`	Not-a-Number	`computer`	Computer type
`i, j`	Imaginary unit ($\sqrt{-1}$)	`nargin`	Number of function input arguments
`eps`	Machine precision	`nargout`	Number of function output arguments
`realmax`	Largest real number		
`realmin`	Smallest real number		

On-line help category: `lang`

A.4   Language Constructs and Debugging

See Section 4.4.

Declarations/Definitions		
`function`	`global`	`nargchk`

Interactive Input Functions		
`input`	`keyboard`	`menu`
`ginput`	`pause`	

Control Flow Functions		
`for`	`elseif`	`break`
`while`	`else`	`error`
`if`	`end`	`return`

Debugging				
`dbclear`	`dbcont`	`dbstep`	`dbstack`	`dbstatus`
`dbup`	`dbdown`	`dbtype`	`dbstop`	`dbquit`

On-line help category: `iofun`

A.5   File I/O

See Section 4.4.7.

File Opening, Closing, and Positioning					
`fopen`	`fclose`	`fseek`	`ftell`	`frewind`	`ferror`

File Reading and Writing					
`fread`	`fwrite`	`fprintf`	`fscanf`	`fgetl`	`fgets`

A.6 Operators and Logical Functions

See Section 3.2.

On-line help category: ops

Arithmetic Operators			
Matrix Operators		*Array Operators*	
+	Addition	+	Addition
–	Subtraction	–	Subtraction
*	Multiplication	.*	Array multiplication
^	Exponentiation	.^	Array exponentiation
/	Left division	./	Array left division
\	Right division	.\	Array right division.

Relational Operators		Logical Operators	
<	Less than	&	Logical AND
<=	Less than or equal	|	Logical OR
>	Greater than	~	Logical NOT
>=	Greater than or equal	xor	Logical EXCLUSIVE OR
==	Equal		
~=	Not equal		

Logical Functions			
all	any	exist	find
finite	isempty	isinf	isnan
isiee	issparse	isstr	

A.7   Math Functions

On-line
help
category:
elfun

See Section 3.2.4 for description and examples.

Trigonometric Functions			
sin	asin	sinh	asinh
cos	acos	cosh	acosh
tan	atan,atan2	tanh	atanh
cot	acot	coth	acoth
sec	asec	sech	asech
csc	acsc	csch	acsch

Exponential Functions			
exp	log	log10	sqrt

Complex Functions		
abs	angle	conj
real	imag	

Round-off Functions			
fix	floor	ceil	round
rem	sign		

Specialized Math Functions			
bessel	besselh	beta	betain
ellipj	ellipke	erf	erfinv
gamma	gammainc	log2	rat

A.8 Matrices: Creation & Manipulation

See Section 3.1.

On-line help category: elmat

Elementary Matrices			
eye	ones	zeros	rand
randn	linspace	logspace	meshgrid

Specialized Matrices			
compan	hadamard	hankel	hilb
invhilb	magic	pascal	rosser
toeplitz	vander	wilkinson	gallery

Matrix Manipulation Functions			
diag	fliplr	flipud	reshape
rot90	tril	triu	:

Matrix (Math) Functions			
expm	logm	sqrtm	funm

Matrix Analysis			
cond	det	norm	null
orth	rank	rref	trace
eig	balance	poly	hess

Matrix Factorization & Inversion			
chol	lu	qr	qz
schur	svd	inv	pinv

Sparse Matrix Functions   There are also several functions for creating, manipulating, and visualizing sparse matrices. Some of these are spdiag, speye, sprandn, full, sparse, spconvert, spalloc, spfun, condest, normest, sprank, gplot and spy. See on-line help for complete listing.

On-line help category: sparfun

A.9   Character String Functions

See Section 3.2.6.

General String Functions			
abs	eval	·isstr	setstr
string	strcmp	lower	upper

String ⟺ Number Conversion			
int2str	num2str	sprintf	hec2hex
str2num	sscanf	hex2dec	hex2num

A.10   Graphics Functions

See Chapter 5.

2-D Graphics				
plot	loglog	semilogx	semilogy	fplot
bar	errorbar	compass	feather	stairs
polar	fill	hist	rose	quiver

3-D Graphics				
plot3	fill3	mesh	meshc	meshz
surf	surfc	surfl	cylinder	sphere

Contour Plots				
contour	contour3	contourc	clabel	pcolor

Graphics Annotation				
xlabel	ylabel	zlabel	title	legend
text	gtext	grid		

Axis Control & Graph Appearance				
axis	colormap	hidden	shading	view

Window Creation & Control				
clf	close	figure	gcf	subplot

Axis Creation & Control				
axes	axis	caxis	cla	gca

Handle Graphics Objects & Operations				
axes	line	patch	surface	text
figure	image	uicontrol	uimenu	
delete	drawnow	get	reset	set

Animation & Movies			
comet	getframe	movie	moviein

Hardcopy & Miscellaneous				
print	orient	printopt	ginput	hold

Color Control & Lighting				
caxis	colormap	flag	hsv2rgb	rgb2hsv
bone	copper	gray	hsv	pink
cool	hot	shading	brighten	diffuse
surfl	specular	rgbplot		

On-line help category:
color

A.11   Applications Functions

On-line
help
category:
datafun

A.11.1   Data analysis and Fourier transforms

Basic Statistics Commands				
mean	median	std	min	max
prod	cumprod	sum	cumsum	sort

Correlation & Finite Difference				
corrcoef	cov	del2	diff	gradient

Fourier Transforms				
fft	fft2	fftshift	ifft	ifft2
abs	angle	cplxpair	nextpow2	unwrap

Filtering & Convolution				
conv	conv2	dconv	filter	filter2

On-line
help
category:
polyfun

A.11.2   Polynomials and data interpolation

Polynomials				
poly	polyder	polyfit	polyval	polyvalm
conv	deconv	residue	roots	

Data Interpolation			
interp1	interp2	interpft	griddata

Fourier Transforms				
fft	fft2	fftshift	ifft	ifft2
abs	angle	cplxpair	nextpow2	unwrap

Filtering & Convolution				
conv	conv2	dconv	filter	filter2

On-line
help
category:
funfun

A.11.3   Nonlinear numerical methods

Functions			
fmin	fmins	fzero	trapz
ode23	ode45	quad	quad8

Bibliography

[1] *MATLAB User's Guide*, The MathWorks, Inc., 1993.

[2] *MATLAB Reference Guide*, The MathWorks, Inc., 1993.

[3] *MATLAB External Interface Guide*, The MathWorks, Inc., 1993.

[4] *MATLAB Building a Graphical User Interface*, The MathWorks, Inc., 1993.

[5] *MATLAB New Features Guide*, The MathWorks, Inc., 1993.

[6] Kernighan B. W. and Ritchie D.M., *The C Programming Language*, second edition, Prentice-Hall Inc., 1993.

Index